MARVELS
of the
TEXAS
PLAINS

MARVELS

of the

TEXAS
PLAINS

Historic Chronicles from the
Courthouse to the Caprock

CHUCK LANEHART

FOREWORD BY MONTE MONROE

THE
History
PRESS

Published by The History Press
Charleston, SC
www.historypress.com

Front cover: Caprock Water, photograph by Ashton Thornhill of Santa Fe, New Mexico.
Back cover, top: photo courtesy of Mary Alice McLarty.

First published 2022

Manufactured in the United States

ISBN 9781467152808

Library of Congress Control Number: 2022939478

This book is dedicated to my grandson, Robert Lee Craig IV, whom I call "Rocky," and to Mom and Dad.

CONTENTS

CONTENTS

FOREWORD

Prominent Lubbock criminal defense attorney Chuck Lanehart, author of the acclaimed *Tragedy and Triumph on the Texas Plains: Curious Historic Chronicles from Murders to Movies*, returns in 2022 with another page-turner. The author's second contribution to the popular and readable The History Press series is entitled *Marvels of the Texas Plains: Historic Chronicles from the Courthouse to the Caprock*. The noted press publishes the works of prominent contemporary and regional historians and others. Similar to his first volume, the new study introduces a crackerjack compilation of articles that Lanehart wrote for the long-running and well-liked *Lubbock Avalanche-Journal* feature Caprock Chronicles.

Lanehart, who proclaims himself a "volunteer writer," is, in actuality, an accomplished essayist of many years and an exceptional storyteller. In publications as different as the *Lubbock Law Notes*, various professional legal journals, collaborations with the late award-winning author Bill Neal of Abilene and innumerable newspaper pieces and public presentations, Lanehart has proven himself a clever, talented and highly proficient lay historian. Though recognized as a preeminent lawyer, his passions and hobbies—besides family and golf—are history and biography. He is an old hand at creating crisp, fast-paced and fascinating stories about crime, law, people, places and often obscure historical events about his native West Texas.

Some thirty-four new historical compositions are well arranged and sequenced into five topical parts in Lanehart's latest work. Each chapter is short and gripping. The narrative morsels live up to the author's trademark "history light" style while providing fresh insights. Lanehart sprinkles adequate details throughout every story to pique curiosity among general readers and stir their interest to delve deeper into the diversity of historical characters and events of the South Plains, eastern New Mexico and the Texas Panhandle regions. From the origins of archaic peoples on the Llano Estacado to legendary buffalo hunters, ranch barons, pioneering land developers, cowboys and the Wild West town of "Old Tascosa," the writer captures his readers' attention. His courthouse tales about irascible attorneys, landmark court decisions and terrible murders are magnetic. A keen student of music, sports and West Texas culture, the author's biographies of regional musicians, sports heroes and actors seduce the bookworm at every turn. Indeed, Lanehart offers up stories for every audience.

His tales are colloquial yet educated, captivating and sometimes peppered with surprise endings. He tramples slightly on a few myths and sacred cows to remind the careful reader of mistakes from our human past. And, as any history junkie can tell you, with so many untold and undertold stories to choose from in the historical past of western Texas, the able Mr. Lanehart will doubtless uncover more yarns worth telling until he rides off into his last blazing prairie sunset. But let us not go there just yet, as certainly more engaging historical and biographical gems will emanate from lawyer Chuck Lanehart's fertile mind for many moons to come. Heck, in this volume, the hilarious "Chappellisms" in part II alone are worth the price of admission.

—Monte L. Monroe
Texas State Historian
Lubbock, Texas

ACKNOWLEDGEMENTS

I applaud the *Lubbock Avalanche-Journal* for publishing Caprock Chronicles on page one of section B of the newspaper every Sunday since 2016. The Chronicles affords volunteer writers like me the opportunity to explore our passion for storytelling. More important, the column presents *A-J* readers vivid accounts of the colorful and important history of our region. Each of the articles contained in this book were originally printed in the Chronicles. My good buddy Jack Becker has done a wonderful job editing the Chronicles, with the able assistance of *A-J* staffer LeAnda Staebner.

The Southwest Collection (SWC) of Texas Tech University is a treasure. Many of the articles presented here could not have been written without the research material available in the Southwest Collection, and several of the photographs in this book were provided by the SWC. I thank archivists Monte Monroe and Weston Marshall of the SWC for their assistance.

My friend and colleague Charles Blevins lent his able technical skills to this effort, producing a nice map to accompany the articles. Legal assistant Bernadette Vaughn—my right hand—formatted the manuscript for publication as she kept me out of trouble with clients and courts. My brother David Lanehart—true historian and trial lawyer extraordinaire—is my sounding board for historical matters, and he is always willing to accompany me on road trips to explore historical sites.

Fred Stangl, my law partner and great friend, should have been a copy editor. He examined almost every article published here for grammar and style. Thanks, Fred.

Finally, my lovely wife, Paula, took time away from her busy duties as an arbitrator, golfer and grandmother to offer sage advice, which greatly improved the storytelling presented in this book.

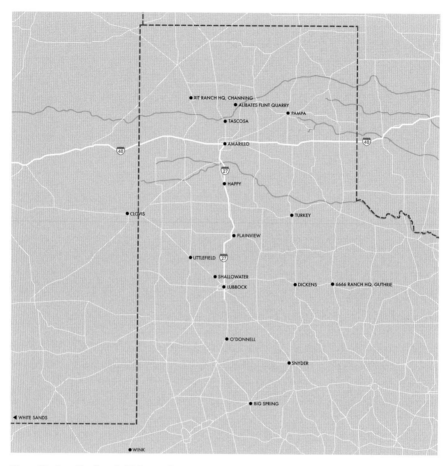

Texas Panhandle, South Plains and eastern New Mexico. *Courtesy of Charles Blevins*.

INTRODUCTION

True tales of the Texas Plains have always intrigued me, but when I started putting these stories down on paper a few years ago, I began to marvel at the depth and breadth of history oozing from the Panhandle and South Plains regions. It seemed to me important events and noteworthy people of the Plains had not been adequately chronicled.

The stories published here were originally written for the *Lubbock Avalanche-Journal's* Caprock Chronicles history column, published every Sunday since 2016. The editors at the *A-J* highly value the space that occupies the column, so I was generally limited to about eight hundred words per article. Thus, these are short, succinct summaries of each subject, not deep dives into historical study. My brother Dave—a true historian—says I write "history light," and he is not wrong.

A good example is the opening chapter published here, about the people who first occupied the Americas. My frugal 805 written words barely scratch the surface, as there are libraries full of important probes into the archaeology, anthropology and history of this intriguing subject. I hope those who are interested in my short chronicle will delve further into the topic.

Other stories are of forgotten or elusive characters of the Texas Plains, like Byron "Lawyer" Chappell, my eccentric mentor and law partner for more than twenty years, and Joe Fortenberry, inventor of the "slam dunk." There are also chronicles of important legal battles, like the prosecution of Cullen Davis, the richest man to stand trial for murder, and *Jones v. the City of Lubbock*, a fight to bring racial diversity to city leadership.

I'm a fan of rock and country music, and the Texas Plains have produced an incredible list of music icons, like Bob Wills, Roy Orbison and Waylon Jennings. They, along with others, are profiled here. When my short bio of O'Donnell's Dan Blocker—aka "Hoss Cartwright"—was published in the *A-J*, I was surprised that it garnered more interest than seemingly all of the dozens of my other Caprock Chronicles, so it is reprinted here. Among the wide range of other eclectic subjects covered here are sports heroes, goofy town names, an unlikely hotel resurrection and a tiny small-town eatery.

I hope my "history light" accounts whet readers' curiosity appetites and spur further reading on these historic chronicles and characters of the Texas Plains.

PART I

TEXAS PLAINS PREHISTORY AND TALES OF THE WILD WEST

FOOTPRINTS IN THE SAND

Was Clovis Man the Earliest American?

For almost a century, artifacts found near Clovis, New Mexico, were accepted by scientists as evidence that the earliest American was Clovis Man, who once flourished on the Texas Plains. However, a recent discovery indicates that earlier humans may have lived nearby, sparking debate about when and how they got there.

In 1927, a cowboy found a mammoth skeleton with a spearpoint in its ribs near Folsom, New Mexico, triggering interest in digging for evidence of early man in the region. Five years later, excavation two hundred miles south in Blackwater Draw near Clovis unearthed projectile points and tools supporting the theory that early humans crossed the Beringia land bridge over the Bering Strait from Siberia to Alaska during the Last Glacial Maximum, a period of lowered sea levels during the Ice Age. Ancient travelers may have made their way southward through an ice-free corridor east of the Rocky Mountains in present-day western Canada as glaciers retreated.

Researchers dubbed the subject of their findings the Clovis Culture, characterized by the beautiful, fluted stone spearpoints crafted by Clovis people and found at sites throughout the Americas.

Clovis people—believed to be ancestors of all Indigenous Americans—spread across the continent between 11,000 and 13,500 years ago. Clovis people foraged and were skilled hunters of big game such as mammoths, mastodons, camels, horses, giant sloths and ancient bison.

The Lubbock Lake Landmark is an archaeological site that preserves evidence of Clovis Culture. Material excavated from an ancient river valley shows evidence that Clovis Man killed and butchered giant Ice Age beasts here.

About eleven thousand years ago, the Clovis Culture abruptly vanished from the archaeological record, and other hunter-gatherer cultures emerged. Their disappearance coincided with the extinction of ancient big-game animals. Did Clovis people overhunt the huge mammals into extinction? Is there another explanation? Conclusive answers may never be found.

After the discovery of Clovis Culture, most scientists accepted the notion that humans first settled the Americas no earlier than about 13,500 years ago by walking from Asia to Alaska via a land bridge. There have been countless claims of earlier humans living as long as 130,000 years ago in the Americas, but virtually all have been called into question.

Now, a new discovery may prove Clovis Man was not the first American. In the early 1930s, a trapper discovered a remarkable footprint—twenty-two inches long and eight inches wide—in the White Sands of New Mexico, west of the Caprock escarpment. The trapper thought he'd found evidence of the mythical Bigfoot, but research confirmed the print was that of a giant sloth. The find spurred further excavation at White Sands.

In recent years, fossilized human footprints were found at White Sands National Park. According to a September 2021 report published in the journal *Science*, the impressions indicate that early humans occupied North America between 21,000 and 23,000 years ago, thousands of years before Clovis Man appeared, transforming views of when—and how—the continent was settled. Dating from a time scientists think massive ice sheets walled off human passage to North America, the fossils seem to prove humans were living in North America before the Last Glacial Maximum closed migration routes from Asia.

Scores of footprints of children and teenagers—and a few adults—formed by walking in soft prehistoric mud were found near ancient Lake Otero, a 1,600-square-mile body of water that dried up about ten thousand years ago and now forms part of Alkali Flat in White Sands. Seeds from Ruppia grass, an aquatic plant, were found in sediment layers above and below the footprints. The seeds were carbon-dated, yielding remarkably precise dates for the impressions.

"One of the reasons there is so much debate is that there is a real lack of very firm, unequivocal data points. That's what we think we probably have [at White Sands]," said Professor Matthew Bennett, an author of the study.

Anthropologists believe the footprints may have been left by youngsters helping adults with a hunting technique seen in later Native American

Fossilized human footprints found at White Sands National Park. *Courtesy of National Park Service.*

cultures, the "buffalo jump," involving driving large game over the edge of a cliff. Butchering of animals began immediately, and fires were started to render fat. Footprints may have been left by teens collecting firewood, water or other essentials during the processing.

The White Sands discovery calls into question not only when humans first arrived on the North American continent but also how. If people were in the Americas during the Last Glacial Maximum, did they arrive through inland routes before the glacial doors slammed shut? Did they boat around icy areas of the coasts? Such questions are the subject of ongoing research at White Sands and elsewhere.

These vestiges of the new oldest Americans were found just a couple hundred miles southwest of the first discovery of Clovis Man, evidence that the Llano Estacado was home to the earliest Americans, regardless of when or how they arrived.

2

THE ALIBATES FLINT QUARRIES

Evidence of the Earliest Humans
of North America

t was 1963. I will never forget my father taking my brother Dave and me, along with other Pampa Boy Scouts, to the Alibates flint quarries near the Canadian River. Scoutmaster Charles Lanehart was a geologist and a student of Native American culture, so he brought us to learn the importance of this historic bit of barren land. He wanted us to see this special Texas Panhandle place, fearful that the new Lake Meredith—which would flood the area a couple of years later—might destroy evidence of the earliest people in the Americas.

Humans may have first reached North America during the Ice Age, about 13,500 years ago, by walking from Asia to what is now Alaska across the frozen Bering Strait. They migrated south and reached what is now the Texas Plains region. There is scant evidence of what these earliest people looked like, what they ate, the homes they lived in or the languages they spoke. The primary traces of human existence on the Llano Estacado thousands of years ago are items they left behind: tools fashioned from small bits of stone.

If he were alive today, Dad would caution that "flint" is technically a silicified or agatized dolomite stone occurring in Permian Age outcroppings, created 250 million years ago. No matter what it is called, Dad would agree that Alibates flint/dolomite is distinguished by a multitude of variations, patterns and vivid colors: pale gray and white to pink, maroon, vivid red, orange gold and intense purplish blue.

This special flint, found only in the ten-square-mile area known as Alibates on the banks and hills surrounding the Canadian River, was the

Pampa Boy Scouts exploring the Alibates Flint Quarry, 1963. The author is pictured with crossed arms. *Photo by Charles Lanehart Sr.*

favored source of stone for early humans manufacturing implements that have been found in abundance throughout the Great Plains, the Southwest and beyond.

Usually buried just below the surface, Alibates flint was commonly dug with quartzite hammers. When shaped properly, the hard Alibates rock was easy to chip and flake into a variety of weapons such as dart points, arrowheads and spears. Tools—knives, hammers, chisels, drills, axes, awls, fishhooks, buttons, hoes and scrapers—were also fashioned from the stone.

Perhaps using nothing more elaborate than a fine antler tip, a chipper might have used a leather pad to protect his hands as he applied pressure on the razor-sharp edge, pushing off one chip at a time, putting the finishing touches on a point before attaching it to a shaft.

Alibates stone was valuable. Prehistoric hunters traveled—or traded—over distances of more than one thousand miles to obtain it. Projectile points and other tools made from Alibates flint have been found as far north as Montana, as far south as Central Mexico and as far east as the Mississippi River.

Small quarry pits and tons of manufacturing debris remain at the site. Archaeologists marvel over the scale and range of prehistoric activities that created this extraordinary spot. Some toolmakers may have just picked up exposed chunks of rock lying on the ground. Others chiseled boulders directly from the bedrock, leaving small holes and broad pits ranging from five to twenty feet across and up to two feet deep. What remains are quarry waste piles and toolmaking debris blanketing the slopes—thousands of quarried chunks, flakes and implements in various stages of production.

Who were these early quarrymen? The earliest Natives of this land were identified as the Clovis Culture, named for their distinctive "points"—projectiles found near Clovis, New Mexico, one hundred years ago. Ancestors of today's Native Americans, Clovis people lived here about thirteen thousand years ago, and used weapons made from Alibates flint to hunt now-extinct large-game animals such as mammoths and ancient bison.

Clovis Man was followed by other prehistoric cultures, including Folsom Man, Plainview Man and others, all of which used Alibates flint for tools and weapons.

Ruins of complex dwellings of a later people, known as the Antelope Creek Culture, lived in the Canadian River area from about AD 1150 to 1450 or later. They shaped Alibates flint for hunting weapons as well as for farming tools, using springs near the river to cultivate beans, corn and squash.

Today, Antelope Creek ruins and flint quarry sites are protected and preserved at the Alibates Flint Quarries National Monument between Amarillo and Fritch. This, the first national monument in Texas, was created by Congress in 1965, thanks to the efforts of the Potter County Historical Survey Committee and concerned individuals, including my father.

Visitors to Alibates Flint Quarries National Monument may trek to the top of the mesa, where flint quarries are located. Park rangers and volunteers lead tours to the quarries, where visitors can see the flint that has been used by humans since the Ice Age. In 2015, Alibates Flint Quarries National Monument celebrated its fiftieth anniversary.

Dad will be smiling next time Dave and I visit the Alibates flint—uh, dolomite—quarries.

3

J. WRIGHT MOOAR AND SNYDER'S LEGENDARY WHITE BUFFALO

Before hide hunters began to penetrate the Great Plains in 1871, sixty million bison—known as buffalo—were thought to occupy the American West. Within a period of eighteen years, just five hundred bison survived perhaps the greatest human slaughter of animals in history. One such kill—that of a white buffalo in Scurry County—is legendary.

Just one in ten million bison is born albino; in humans, the rate is perhaps one in twenty thousand. Only seven white buffalo were reported taken by Anglo hunters—and just one in Texas.

To Native Americans, the buffalo is a symbol of sacred life and abundance. Indians relied on bison for their very existence, using every part of the animal for food, shelter and tools. The birth of a revered white buffalo is a sign of hope, an indication of good times to come and the most significant of prophetic signs, similar to miracles of the Christian faith.

To frontiersmen looking ever westward, the buffalo was an important source of commerce. Buffalo were first hunted for meat, but soon tanned buffalo hides became valuable. Later, bison bones were used for fertilizer. The slaughter of bison also served to deprive Plains tribes of their sustenance, helping to force Indians onto reservations to make way for cattle where buffalo once roamed.

J. Wright Mooar was born in Vermont in 1851. By age twenty, he was hunting buffalo in Kansas. In 1873, Wright—joined by his brother John and William "Pete" Snyder—ventured into the Panhandle of Texas, rich with huge herds of bison. It was a risky undertaking, as hostile Comanches occupied the area.

John Mooar (*left*) and J. Wright Mooar display the hide of the white buffalo Wright killed near Snyder on October 7, 1876. *Courtesy of the Scurry County Museum.*

Wright led a group of hide men south into Scurry County in the fall of 1876. Hunting alone near Deep Creek on October 7, Wright paused on a hillside to gaze over the beautiful country below the Caprock. He saw a small herd of buffalo, and something glistened in the evening sun. He rode closer: it was a white buffalo!

He hurried to camp, about a mile away, and recruited the assistance of a buffalo skinner, Dan Dowd. They rode toward the herd, tied their horses some distance away and crawled closer. The magnificent beast was sighted among about four thousand others.

Raising his powerful "Big Fifty" Sharps rifle to his shoulder, Wright aimed and felled the great animal with one shot. The herd stampeded toward the two men, and Wright killed three bulls to avoid being trampled.

Wright enjoyed great acclaim throughout the frontier region for his feat, and his white buffalo pelt was displayed at the 1904 St. Louis World's Fair. Teddy Roosevelt offered Wright $5,000 for the albino bison's hide, but the offer was declined. The famed buffalo hunter established a ranch in Scurry County, becoming one of the first to settle the area. Soon, the town of Snyder was established nearby. He married Julia Swartz and adopted a son.

Wright—said to have slaughtered more than twenty-two thousand bison in his career—was criticized as a ruthless killer and wastrel of a great game resource. But he was unapologetic.

> *Buffalo hunting was a business, not a sport; it required capital, management and work, lots of hard work, more work than anything else. Many magazines and newspaper articles claim the killing of the buffalo a national calamity and accomplished by vandals. I resent their ignorance.*
>
> *The buffalo hunter lived with and on the buffalo…had plenty of ammunition to spare and a vastly superior gun to anything the Indian had ever met. Buffalo hunting opened up a vast empire of territory for occupation, put the Indian forever out of Texas, changed him from a blood-thirsty savage to a meek, submissive ward.*
>
> *The cow men ever quick and alert to see opportunity followed in the wake of the buffalo hunters so closely many large herds of cattle were located in hearing of the roar of the Big Fifty's. So when the buffalo was exterminated, the country was stocked with cattle.*
>
> *Any one of the many families killed and homes destroyed by the Indians would have been worth more to Texas and civilization than all of the millions of buffalo that ever roamed from the Pecos River on the South to the Platte River on the North.*

Wright died at age eighty-nine in 1940, and 3,500 mourners attended his funeral in Snyder. The white hide remains in the possession of Wright's Scurry County descendants.

A statue of a white bull buffalo was erected in 1967 on the Scurry County Courthouse square to commemorate Wright's great accomplishment. However, someone noticed that the white buffalo hide on display at Wright's ranch was not that of a bull. It was a bison cow, about four years old.

In 1994, the original statue was replaced by a bronze statue of a female white buffalo. It continues to greet visitors to downtown Snyder.

Thanks to conservation efforts, five hundred thousand buffalo now populate America.

4

THOMAS SALTUS LUBBOCK

What's in a Name?

Texas legislators of 1876 must not have considered the man's character when they named a desolate, empty, flat plat of grassland on the Plains in honor of Thomas S. Lubbock. Not much was known of the man, then or now. He was briefly a soldier in the Texas Revolution, a failed campaigner for the Republic of Texas and a military officer of the Confederacy. He was also a slaveholder and a member of a malevolent secret society.

Thomas Saltus Lubbock was born in Charleston, South Carolina, in 1817. By 1835, he was a teenaged cotton broker in New Orleans. This is a coincidental bit of history: the county that bears Lubbock's name lies at the center of the largest contiguous cotton patch in the world.

When the Texas Revolution began, he joined a company of the New Orleans Greys and marched to Nacogdoches, then to San Antonio, where he participated in the 1835 siege of Bexar, the first major military campaign of the rebellion.

Lubbock saw no further action in the Texas War for Independence, but he remained in Texas, working on a Brazos River steamboat. This random fragment of Lubbock's biography is also noteworthy, as the Brazos has its headwaters on Blackwater Draw, which passes through Lubbock County just north of the city of Lubbock.

Following independence, the impoverished Republic of Texas coveted the trade potential of the Santa Fe Trail region and claimed huge sections of what is now New Mexico. A coalition of 321 businessmen, soldiers and politicians embarked on what became known as the Santa Fe Expedition, hoping to persuade Mexicans of the area to submit to Texas authority.

Lubbock joined the group, which left the Texas Hill Country in June 1841. The expedition—with twenty-one ox-drawn wagons—had difficulty scaling the Caprock Escarpment in what is now Motley County. They eventually crossed the Quitaque and Tule Canyons and reached Laguna Colorada near present-day Tucumcari on October 5. On this route, the expedition must have passed just north of what is now Lubbock County, so Lubbock may have traveled within fifty miles of what would become his namesake county.

Upon reaching Laguna Colorada, the Mexican army captured the entire expeditionary force. Lubbock and his fellow prisoners were marched to Mexico City, where he was confined in Santiago Convent. Lubbock escaped by jumping from the convent's balcony and made his way home to Texas in 1842.

In a time of peace before the Civil War, Lubbock made his living from agribusiness. In 1843, he married Sarah Obedience Smith in Houston, and they had seven children. He was described as a "small and affable" man who "made a favorable impression," and his property was valued at $70,000 ($2.5 million in today's dollars).

At the beginning of the Civil War in 1861, Lubbock left Galveston with Benjamin Franklin Terry and others to join the Confederate cause. In Virginia, Lubbock and Texas volunteers scouted for the Confederate army. He participated in an attack on a Union camp, capturing a couple of Union soldiers, a horse and a Sharps rifle.

Terry and Lubbock were asked to recruit a regiment of cavalry in Texas, and it became known as Terry's Texas Rangers. The regiment returned to the front, with Colonel Terry in command and Lubbock as lieutenant colonel. Terry was killed in the December 1861 Battle of Woodsonville, in Kentucky, and in January 1862, Lubbock died of typhus in a friend's Tennessee home. He was forty-four years old.

Census records show that Lubbock owned thirty-one slaves in 1860. He was a strong secessionist and a "very worthy and zealous" member of the Knights of the Golden Circle, along with Jefferson Davis and other Southern leaders. The Knights of the Golden Circle was a secretive organization established in 1854.

The Knights schemed to create a 2,400-square-mile slaveholding empire to include the southern United States, the West Indies, Mexico and parts of Central America, hoping to preserve slavery and corner the world's supply

Thomas Saltus Lubbock, painting by Bruce Marshall of Austin. *Courtesy of the Southwest Collection, Texas Tech University.*

of tobacco, sugar and cotton. Texans supported the movement, and local Knight chapters were organized in many Texas communities. The end of the Civil War dashed the Knights' plans.

There are no statues of Lubbock, but near the west entrance to the Lubbock County Courthouse stands a granite monument that commemorates Lubbock's service to the Confederacy. The west side of the monument includes a racially insensitive and disingenuous memorial to "Texas in the Civil War." The monument is dated 1964, an era when Confederate monuments were erected in public places by local governments in the South to intimidate Black people and discourage the civil rights movement.

What's in a name? Residents are proud Lubbock County is the agricultural, educational and medical hub of West Texas, the renowned hometown of music legends and other cultural icons. It is unfortunate that the community cannot take such pride in the story of its namesake, Thomas Saltus Lubbock.

5
THE LEGENDARY 6666 RANCH

The legend that the Four Sixes was won with a poker hand of four sixes is unfounded, but that does not make the tale of this iconic Texas ranch any less legendary. In 1867, seventeen-year-old Samuel Burk Burnett drove a herd of his father's Texas longhorns to Kansas. With his earnings, he purchased a herd of one hundred cattle bearing the 6666 brand from Frank Crowley in Denton County. He first recorded the brand in Wichita County in 1875, but the mark's origin remains a mystery.

Burnett's ranching ventures began in Wichita County in about 1870, then shifted to the Red River, and later he leased land on the Comanche-Kiowa Reservation. The lease agreement led to a lifelong friendship with Comanche chief Quanah Parker and an appreciation for Native American culture. When the federal government threatened to cancel the lease, Burnett met with President Theodore Roosevelt and negotiated an extension on his lease. The two bonded, and in 1906, Roosevelt joined Burnett and Parker on a ten-day wolf hunt on the reservation.

In 1900, he finalized his purchase of the 140,000-acre Old Eight Ranch in King County with 1,500 head of stock and moved his 6666 Ranch headquarters to Guthrie. He acquired ranchland in Carson and Hutchinson Counties, called the Dixon Creek Division. Within a few years, Burnett owned a third of a million acres of ranchland.

By culling cows and importing purebred Hereford and Durham bulls, Burnett gradually improved his stock. The resultant offspring became consistent winners as feeder cattle in livestock shows nationwide.

A 1906 wolf hunt, Indian Territory. Participants included Quanah Parker, Burk Burnett and Theodore Roosevelt. *Public domain.*

In 1917, Burnett built a magnificent $100,000 stone ranch house—the "Big House"—on a hill overlooking Guthrie, with barns, corrals, a bunkhouse and other outbuildings erected around it. The next year, a severe Panhandle blizzard killed two thousand cattle on the Dixon Creek Division, but the losses were soon forgotten when oil and gas reserves were discovered beneath Burnett's Carson County ranchland.

After Burnett's death in 1922, the Four Sixes passed via trust to his granddaughter, the tall, attractive Anne Burnett Tandy. Affectionately called "Miss Anne," she was known for her knowledge of cattle, horses and fine art. She established the $200 million Burnett foundation in 1978 to support projects ranging from horse ranching to museums. Nationally known as a judge and breeder of champion racers and show horses, she was instrumental in the organization of the American Quarter Horse Association.

The Four Sixes won fame as a setting for Marlboro cigarette television ads during the 1960s, with ranch employees posing as the iconic "Marlboro Man." In 1975, the Roy Rogers movie *Mackintosh and T.J.* was filmed at the ranch, and the ranch has been the subject of paintings by area artists. One of the original red 6666 barns, for years a prominent landmark in Guthrie, is now on the grounds of Lubbock's Ranching Heritage Center.

In recent years, the Four Sixes began the crossbreeding of Brangus cattle with ranch Herefords to produce the Black Baldie, a hardy breed more resilient to cedar flies, a common pest in the cedar breaks of West Texas. Champion quarter horses continue to reap profits for the Four Sixes.

Land conservation is a continuing tradition. "What struck me about spending time on the Four Sixes was how close to pristine prairie this land is," says the author of *6666: Portrait of a Texas Ranch*, Henry Chappell. "They spend nearly as much time clearing pastures and fighting back mesquite to enhance the land as they do tending their horses and cattle. Even in the present day, the rolling plains, the canyons and the abundance of wildlife all unite to make you feel you have stepped into the past, where buffalo hunters or Comanche warriors could appear at any moment over the next rise."

Miss Anne's daughter Anne Windfohr Marion, known as "Little Anne"—Burk's great-granddaughter—inherited the Burnett fortune and the Four Sixes when her mother died in 1980. Described as "statuesque, strikingly beautiful, regal of bearing and quick of wit, and as hard-working as any of her ranch hands," she was a shrewd businessperson, horsewoman and philanthropist, and she enjoyed quail hunting on the Four Sixes. She served on the Texas Tech University Board of Regents and received the National Golden Spur Award from the National Ranching Heritage Center at Tech.

"The most important thing that ever happened to me was growing up on that ranch," Little Anne said. "It kept my feet on the ground more than anything else."

After Anne Marion's death in 2020, the Four Sixes was advertised for sale for an asking price of $347.7 million. Western screenwriter and producer Taylor Sheridan (*Yellowstone*, *1883*, *Hell or High Water*), representing a buying group, purchased the property in May 2021 for just under $200 million, according to news accounts.

For the first time in 150 years, Burk Burnett's ranches will be operated by someone other than a Burnett family member.

6

THE XIT WAS THE WORLD'S LARGEST CATTLE RANCH

The largest U.S. state spawned the world's largest cattle ranch to build the largest U.S. state capitol building. In 1879, Texas lawmakers saw the need for a much bigger capitol, so they traded a huge tract of public land in the western Panhandle to fund the project. The land became the gargantuan XIT Ranch—more than three million acres stretching two hundred miles across Dallam, Hartley, Oldham, Deaf Smith, Parmer, Castro, Bailey, Lamb, Cochran and Hockley Counties.

Investors in the project became known as the "Capitol Syndicate," led by Chicago brothers Charles and John Farwell (namesakes of the Parmer County seat). They raised more than $3 million to pay for the bulk of construction costs for the new capitol—still the largest capitol building in the United States—completed in 1888.

Meanwhile, additional funds were raised to fence the ranch, build houses and barns, erect windmills and purchase cattle. The Syndicate intended to run cattle only until the land could be utilized for private agriculture. They hoped to promote settlement, eventually subdivide the acreage and gradually sell it off piecemeal.

In 1885, Ab Blocker delivered the first longhorns to ranch manager "Barbeque" Campbell. Blocker demonstrated how to apply five strokes with a straight-line branding iron to create the XIT brand, a mark difficult for rustlers to alter. Some say the meaning of XIT is "ten in Texas," a reference to the number of counties the ranch covered. Others say it means "biggest in Texas."

Campbell found it impossible to control the sprawling ranch, and it became a haven for rustlers and outlaws. Albert Boyce, "a frontier cowman of commanding presence and vast experience," became ranch manager in 1888. He fired and replaced the ranch's 150 cowboys and substituted Hereford, Angus and other purebred stock for the longhorns.

Boyce reorganized operations, dividing the venture into eight sections: Buffalo Springs, Middle Water, Ojo Bravo, Alamasitas, Rita Blanca, Escarbada, Spring Lake and Yellow Houses. Each had a separate function. He established ranch headquarters in the town of Channing, where he built a home and general office building.

Between 1886 and the late 1890s, 1,500 miles of barbed wire were in place to divide the land into ninety-four pastures. By 1887, between 125,000 and 150,000 cattle were occupying the range, about twenty acres per head. Water was provided by 335 tall windmills and 100 earthen dams.

Cowboys and other XIT employees were encouraged to exhibit "sterling honesty and integrity." Written rules prohibited them from carrying firearms, drinking alcohol, gambling, abusing stock or killing beef without permission.

XIT cowboys, circa 1881. Courtesy of the Portal to Texas History.

Nevertheless, lawlessness was common in the region. Billy the Kid and other cattle thieves ventured east from New Mexico, and the wild cow town of Tascosa in Oldham County offered many distractions for XIT men: saloons, brothels, gambling and gun violence.

At the peak of the XIT's operations, 150 cowboys rode 1,000 horses and branded 35,000 calves in one year. For eleven consecutive years, 12,500 cattle were driven annually to northern pastures of the ranch and fattened for the Chicago markets.

Despite excellent ranch management, the operation showed little profit most years. Cattle prices crashed in 1886 and 1887. Cattle rustling, droughts, blizzards, prairie fires and the predatory Mexican wolf led to further losses.

By the late 1890s, the Syndicate began selling out. George Littlefield (namesake of the Lamb County seat) was the first large purchaser, buying 235,858 acres for his LIT Ranch. Other large ventures cut out of the XIT were the Mashed O, Bravo and JJ Ranches. By 1905, much of the land had been divided into small tracts and sold to farmers. The last of the XIT cattle were sold in 1912, and the last parcel of XIT land was sold in 1963.

Prominent Panhandle attorney Temple Houston, Sam Houston's youngest son, dedicated the new Texas Capitol on May 16, 1888, with his famous oratory before a crowd of thousands in Austin.

> *The people of Texas are indebted to* [the Farwells]…*for bringing our public lands into worldwide notice.…They have obtained 3,000,000 acres of the best land in Texas and will in due time cover them with prosperous farmers and increase the wealth of the state by hundreds of millions of dollars.*
>
> *Every true and honest Texan must rejoice that the Farwells have found a way to turn our previously useless land into such a state monument as we are this day dedicating, and that they must from self-interest—if no other motive—cover these lands with farmers as soon as railroads have opened them up. From every point of view…we have done better than any of us thought, and the Farwells are justly entitled to our thanks.*

The XIT general office and manager's residence still stand in Channing. The restored Escarbada division headquarters building can be seen today at the National Ranching Heritage Center in Lubbock.

7

TASCOSA

Toughest Town of the Wild West

Frontier cow towns of the late 1800s are remembered for violence, gambling, womanizing, drunkenness and lawlessness—places like Dodge City, Tucson, Abilene and Lincoln. But the short-lived Texas Panhandle town of Tascosa epitomized the wildest notions of the Old West.

The area, in what is now Oldham County, is located near a crossing of the Canadian River. After the U.S. Army forced Native Americans out of Texas in 1876, the Panhandle's vast treeless plains, covered with lush native grasses, attracted cattlemen, sheep ranchers, land speculators, bison hunters—and outlaws.

The first to arrive was a Comanchero (Indian trader) from New Mexico. Casimero Romero settled his family and one hundred laborers near Atascosa Creek with a herd of three thousand sheep. The closest civilization was a four-day horse ride to Mobeetie, in Wheeler County, 120 miles away.

The village was named Atascosa, Spanish for "boggy," but Anglo Americans who arrived later changed it to Tascosa, the name eventually recognized by the U.S. Post Office. Tascosa became the "Cowboy Capital of the Plains," a trading center for giant ranches: the LX, LIT, LS, XIT and Frying Pan. Pioneer merchants arrived to support ranchers, farmers and dairymen.

Tascosa was a magnet for cowboys seeking entertainment. They were soon joined by others who sought to benefit from the cowboys' many vices. Saloonkeepers, gamblers, con men, prostitutes and dance-hall girls, no longer tolerated by more settled locales, all came to Tascosa—and with good reason.

Interior of a Tascosa saloon, circa 1880s. *Courtesy of the Southwest Collection, Texas Tech University.*

For its first few years, Tascosa had no government and no lawmen. The only law was gun law. It was a town where drinking, gambling and prostitution were common any time of the day or night.

Two districts separated the village. The disreputable eastern portion was known as Hogtown, where "the inhabitants behaved like swine and came away from there hog drunk," according to a former Tascosa resident. A sign at the boundary declared, "No Shooting beyond This Line."

Vice flourished in all forms. Backrooms of saloons did big business. Rowdy Kate was queen of the Hogtown district, and her girls were known as Midnight Rose, Panhandle Nan, Fickle Flossie, Old Ella, Rag-Time Annie, Drowsy Dollie, Crippled Callie and Box-Car Jane.

Tascosa was named county seat in 1880, and an $18,000 courthouse was constructed, but except for the majestic stone edifice, it was a town of tents and adobe. Even after lawmen appeared, drinking, gambling, prostitution and violence persisted.

Before the culmination of the Lincoln County War in New Mexico in 1881, desperado William H. Bonney—"Billy the Kid"—wandered into Tascosa with four companions to sell and trade a number of horses, probably stolen. The Kid made many friends, who noted his excellent behavior, but Bonney's behavior was not the norm in Tascosa.

Gunplay often arose during drunken disputes over card games and women, and more sober disputes arose over land ownership and cattle. An estimated half million cattle were said to have been rustled in the Panhandle during the 1880s. Tascosa's "Boot Hill" sprang up, the final resting place for more than thirty victims of violence in the first six years of the town's history. One of the first to be buried there was a lawman, Oldham County deputy sheriff Henry McCullar.

In 1882, McCullar was shot and killed by Frank Larque, alias Mexican Frank. Larque, a twenty-two-year-old gambler, was tried for murder and sentenced to twenty-two years in prison. This was the first court victory for law and order in Tascosa. Despite a brief escape from prison, Larque was pardoned in 1896 and released.

Bill Gibson occupied another gravesite at Boot Hill. Drunk at a Hogtown saloon, he openly displayed a large roll of bills. He was found dead in a side room the next day. Prosecutors alleged that bartender John Maley and dance-hall girl Sally Emory lured him into the room to sleep off his intoxication, then robbed Gibson and killed him. They were tried for the crime but acquitted for lack of evidence.

Gun battles of the Old West like the "Shootout at the OK Corral" are familiar subjects of Western literature and film. Another compelling story— almost forgotten—is the "Big Fight" in Tascosa, which resulted in more deaths than those at the OK Corral.

The Tascosa shootout began when a bartender and a former Texas Ranger clashed over the affections of a dance-hall girl. But the roots of the controversy are more complicated than a common romantic rivalry.

Cattle ranching, the lifeblood of cow towns like Tascosa, was changing. The cowboy was no longer the quintessential American hero, the self-reliant icon of the plains.

With the coming of the "beef bonanza," the cowboy now worked for huge cattle syndicates. Once an independent small entrepreneur, the cowboy was now a corporate employee working for slim wages with long hours.

Resentment led to the Panhandle cowboy strike of 1883. Striking cowboys hung around Tascosa for a few weeks, but the ranching syndicates refused to budge. The strike collapsed, the strikers were blacklisted and they found themselves without work. They joined a rustling operation led by Tascosa saloonkeeper Jesse Jenkins called "The System," aka "The Get Even Cattle Company."

Soon, the big cattlemen offered Pat Garrett—the lawman who three years earlier had killed Billy the Kid in New Mexico Territory—$5,000 a year to lead a quasi–Texas Rangers unit dubbed the LS Rangers (for their ties to the sprawling LS Ranch) to stamp out the rustlers. Garrett quit after about nine months, but his Rangers continued to work for the LS and loitered in Tascosa taverns, reviled as "barroom gladiators." Former Texas Ranger and LS Ranger Ed King was known as a particularly quarrelsome drunk.

Supporters of The System included Len Woodruff, bartender for Jesse Jenkins' saloon, Louis "the Animal" Bousman, Charlie "Squirrel-Eye" Emory and John "the Catfish Kid" Gough.

Trouble started when King and other Rangers taunted Woodruff, calling him "Pretty Len" and slapping his face. King added insult to injury when he won the favor of Len's lover, dance-hall girl Sally Emory.

After midnight on March 21, 1886, King appeared at the Equity Bar in Tascosa with Rangers Frank Valley, Fred Chilton and John Lang.

Chaos and gunplay followed. Survivors disagreed on details of the Big Fight, but here's what probably happened.

King, Lang and Sally left the Equity and approached Jenkins' saloon. Someone called King's name, a shot rang out and King fell, blood gushing from his mouth. As Sally ran for safety, Len bolted from the saloon, jammed the barrel of a Winchester against King's neck and pulled the trigger before retreating inside.

Saloon and hotel, Tascosa, circa 1870s. *Courtesy of the Southwest Collection, Texas Tech University.*

Lang, who witnessed the shooting, ran into the Equity. He yelled to Chilton and Valley, "They've killed Ed! Come on!" The trio dashed across the square to Jenkins' bar, where Len, Squirrel-Eye, the Catfish Kid and the Animal were holed up.

Valley charged into Jenkins' saloon, guns blazing. Len took two bullets, one through his belly, the other in the groin, and Squirrel-Eye went down with a chunk shot out of his leg. Both survived. Len staggered to the rear of the saloon and fell inside, closing a door behind him.

Valley fired several shots through the door, then pushed it open. A rifle fired, and Valley fell dead on the spot, shot through the left eye. About the same time, innocent bystander Jesse Sheets peered out the back door of a restaurant, and either Chilton or Lang shot him dead. A second later, rifle fire from the woodpile at the rear of the building cut Chilton down.

Lang, the only Ranger survivor, fled under a hail of bullets as Sheriff Jim East and his deputy, Charlie Pierce, came running. As the lawmen passed Lang, the Catfish Kid darted from behind the woodpile. Pierce ordered him to stop, but he kept running, so the deputy fired, and the Catfish Kid went down. Pierce left him for dead, but the Catfish Kid was playing possum and ran off without a scratch. The battle lasted less than five minutes.

Four men lay dead: Rangers King, Valley and Chilton, along with innocent bystander Sheets. Sheriff East took the precaution of closing all the saloons, and townspeople peacefully buried the Rangers at Boot Hill. Sheets' widow buried him elsewhere.

Lang, Woodruff, Bousman, Emory and Gough were indicted for murder by an Oldham County grand jury. Their cases were transferred to Wheeler County on a change of venue, but many court records have been lost. It is believed all defendants were cleared by acquittal, hung jury or court dismissal.

Some historians regard the Big Fight as little more than a drunken brawl, but it was simultaneously the high point and low point of the undeclared war between the cattle syndicates and the rustlers, a war that would rage another decade or more.

In 1887, the Fort Worth and Denver Railway bypassed Tascosa because of the deep, sandy terrain nearby. The town—with a population never to exceed six hundred souls—began to fade. Homes and businesses were damaged by flood in 1893, and people began to move away. The last residents were ex-gambler Mickey McCormick and his wife, former dance-hall girl Frenchy. Mickey died in 1912. Frenchy—the last of the Tascosans—left in 1939 and died in 1941. The two are buried side by side, not on Boot Hill, but in the Casimero Romero Cemetery outside of town.

In 1913, prominent Amarillo rancher and oilman Lee Bivens purchased the LIT Ranch, including the ghost town of Tascosa. In 1939, Bivens' son Lee donated the townsite to charity, and Cal Farley's Boys Ranch became a reality the same year. The courthouse, now a museum, and the 1889 schoolhouse are the only Tascosa buildings that have survived into the twenty-first century.

PART II

HISTORIC LAWYERS AND LAWSUITS OF THE TEXAS PLAINS

8

LAWYERS WERE PART OF LUBBOCK'S EARLY DEVELOPMENT

When the village of Lubbock, Texas, was settled in the 1890s, there was no shortage of lawyers. In a community of fewer than three hundred residents, Lubbock County was home to as many as nine lawyers, 3 percent of the population. If the same percentage held true today, Lubbock lawyers would number eight thousand. We have about eight hundred.

Despite the abundance of attorneys in Lubbock's early years, few lawsuits were filed. Ten civil actions were filed in county court between 1891 and 1900. Without legal secretaries, lawyers were obliged to write all pleadings in longhand. No typewritten documents appeared before 1900 in Lubbock court records.

The district judge's job was tough. By 1891, Lubbock County was part of the thirteen-county Fiftieth Judicial District, stretching from Seymore to New Mexico.

Judge W.R. McGill traveled from courthouse to courthouse in a wagon with three dogs for company. One day, he tired of two lawyers and their poor legal arguments. He sat a dog on the bench, and the judge moved to the gallery. One of the lawyers continued to address the judge in the gallery, but the lawyer who addressed the dog won the case.

Itinerant trial lawyers who followed the judge from town to town became known as "prairie dog lawyers." They often had no formal offices, practicing law from the flatbed of a buggy or out of the back room of a saloon.

Three lawyers practiced in Lubbock County at the time of its organization, Connie Henderson, Will Hendrix and Robert E. Lee Rogers. Henderson is considered the first plaintiff's lawyer—he filed the first lawsuit in county court and four of the first ten in district court.

Henderson represented the first person tried in Lubbock County for a felony crime. Defendant Jim Vance, described as just a boy, was accused of horse theft in June 1891. Vance told the jury he took the mare but left a note to the horse owner: "They are after me for killing two Mexicans. My horse broke down, and I think you would let me have yours if you was here. I will send her back or give you $60." Vance apparently never paid for the horse or brought it back, but he was acquitted.

Hendrix, the first county attorney of Lubbock County, handled the first lawsuit filed in district court, a suit for debt. It seems the defendant had not paid the plaintiff for building a one-and-one-half-story hotel. The price contracted for building the hotel was $114.50.

Rogers, the second county attorney of Lubbock County, published the first newspaper, the *Lubbock Leader*. The short-lived paper carried advertising

Law office of J.J. Dillard, Lubbock, circa 1900. *Courtesy of the Southwest Collection, Texas Tech University.*

for Henderson and Hendrix. Like today's lawyers, those in the 1890s were not shy about promoting themselves.

Henderson touted himself as an "attorney at law, notary public, collection agent, abstractor, creator of surveys promptly and accurately made on short notice—prices reasonable." Hendrix represented himself as "attorney at law and insurance agent, Lubbock, Texas. Has for sale and lease 25 sections of land on easy terms."

These early Lubbock lawyers were of the wandering prairie dog type. They didn't stick around very long. The second generation began their practices about the turn of the century, as Lubbock was about to become a boomtown.

The new lawyers stayed and prospered. In 1902, W.D. Benson arrived with his family in a covered wagon. As a young man, Benson was a cowboy. He was given a used copy of *Blackstone's Commentaries*, and with the aid of a dictionary, he studied law when not punching cows. After a period of study, he appeared before the district judge, ready to be given his oral bar exam.

The judge admitted that he had never given a bar exam and didn't know the proper questions. Finally, the judge improvised an inquiry: "Mr. Benson, give me the definition of *habeas corpus*."

Benson apologized and told the judge he didn't know the meaning of *habeas corpus*. With that, the judge declared Benson a duly qualified attorney. "Mr. Benson, I can't honestly say that I understand what it means either, so I guess you pass."

Benson established what was considered Lubbock's first modern law office on the block where the federal building now stands. He employed the first stenographer, used the first typewriter and maintained the first law library in Lubbock.

Attorney John J. Dillard, later justice of the peace, in 1900 cofounded, published and edited the *Lubbock Avalanche*, predecessor of the *Lubbock Avalanche-Journal*.

In 1893, George R. Bean came to Lubbock as a teenager with his family and lived at first in a dugout. Licensed as an attorney in 1901, Bean founded what eventually became Jones, Flygare, Brown and Wharton—one of Lubbock's oldest law firms.

Benson, Dillard and Bean each had sons who practiced law in Lubbock well into the twentieth century. Benson's grandson Dan was an esteemed Texas Tech law professor until his death in 2011.

9

WHO SHOT THE SHERIFF?

The South Plains Trial of the Century

In the winter of 1935, two trials dominated South Plains newspaper headlines. The celebrated New Jersey trial of Richard Hauptmann for the kidnapping and murder of the Lindbergh baby became known as the "Trial of the Century." But on the South Plains, Hauptmann news coverage was overshadowed by the Lubbock trial of Virgil Stalcup, accused of murdering the Dickens County sheriff.

Stalcup was born in New Mexico in 1907. He was small—five feet, six inches tall and 140 pounds—with fair complexion, green eyes and balding light brown hair. Described as "pug-nosed," he sported a gold-capped front tooth and smoked constantly. He was married at age twenty, and the couple had a daughter. Stalcup found work as an auto mechanic but soon embarked on a more lucrative, brief, intense life of crime.

His specialty was armed robbery, stealing from victims throughout the Southwest. At age twenty-three, Stalcup landed in the Texas penitentiary, serving 125 years for robberies out of Wilbarger, Potter and Wichita Counties.

On April 13, 1934, Stalcup escaped from prison and made his way to the home of his father—O.B. Stalcup—near Lawton, Oklahoma. There, he hooked up with thirty-eight-year-old Clarence Brown of Snyder. They pulled off a string of robberies in Oklahoma, New Mexico and Texas.

When authorities closed in on O.B.'s home on June 17, there was a shootout. Stalcup was shot in the shoulder, and his fifty-four-year-old father was killed. Two police officers were wounded by gunfire, and Stalcup and Brown surrendered.

Dickens County sheriff Bill Arthur. *Courtesy of the Spur-Dickens County Museum.*

After their arrest, Stalcup and Brown confessed to a number of crimes. Both were transferred to Dickens County to face trial for the robbery of a bottling company truck driver. Stalcup was transferred to Lamb County for a plea of guilty to a Littlefield robbery. After the judge sentenced him to a ten-year prison term, Stalcup told the judge he "had no intentions of serving the sentence." He was returned to Dickens County.

The Dickens County sheriff was forty-three-year-old Bill Arthur. Born in New Mexico in 1886, he moved to Dickens County as a young man. He married Nannie Stegall in 1908, and the couple had six children. In 1931, he was elected sheriff, and the family moved into the first-floor living quarters of the 1909 Dickens County Jail. Prisoners were housed on the second floor of the quaint stone structure.

In mid-July 1934, the sheriff confronted W.J. "Jenks" Yarbrough in McAdoo. Yarbrough, a forty-year-old farmer, was suspected of illegally carrying a handgun. Yarbrough pulled his .25 caliber pistol and shot Sheriff Arthur five times. The sheriff did not fall. He pulled his pistol and fired but missed as the shooter fled. Arthur walked to a nearby icehouse and told the proprietor, "Let's go to the hospital."

He was treated at a Lubbock sanitarium, but doctors were unable to remove four bullets lodged in the sheriff's thigh, buttocks and chest. Nevertheless, the sheriff was soon well enough to resume his duties.

His wife, Nannie, told the sheriff he should find another line of work. "I had rather pick cotton—anything," she said. But her sound advice was ignored.

Yarbrough was soon arrested and taken to the Dickens County Jail, housed in a cell adjacent to Stalcup and Brown.

On August 18, Stalcup and Brown—brandishing a knife—escaped from the jail. Within days, Brown was recaptured at his home in Snyder and returned to the Dickens County Jail. His attractive, twenty-seven-year-old wife, Thelma, often traveled to see her husband in the hoosegow. On one such visit, she charmed jailers and smuggled a pistol into the jail. The gun would later factor into the killing of the Dickens County sheriff.

Stalcup remained free for a couple of months. In the badlands near Clarendon, the outlaw was spotted by a large posse of well-armed lawmen. During a wild ten-mile car-and-foot chase, deputies fired at him with machine guns. He was captured unharmed on October 23 and was returned to Dickens County. During his two months on the lam, Stalcup had committed robberies in at least three Texas counties. A reporter wrote that he faced 254 years in prison.

Just four days later, the commode on the second floor of the jail overflowed. The layout of the tiny, five-cell jail required the sheriff to enter the cellblock in order to examine the problem with the toilet.

Stalcup and Brown played cards in the southeast cage as Yarbrough read in the northeast cage, closest to the commode. Apparently, none of the cell doors were locked. The sheriff knelt over the commode to repair the plumbing. Suddenly, a shot rang out. Sheriff Arthur stumbled into Yarbrough's cell and fell to his knees by the cot, mortally wounded by a bullet to his neck.

Stalcup and Brown were gone, along with the sheriff's weapons and car. Investigators suspected that Arthur had carelessly entered the cellblock armed and was killed with his own pistol.

A nationwide manhunt for Sheriff Arthur's alleged murderers—Stalcup and Brown—paused on October 30 for the sheriff's funeral. More than five thousand mourners, including dozens of law-enforcement personnel from several states, attended.

Four days later, both desperados were arrested near Houston without incident. "I guess this is the last break I'll ever make," Stalcup said.

Talk of vigilante justice in Dickens meant the duo would be housed in the more secure Lubbock County Jail. Stalcup and Brown were indicted for capital murder. Stalcup's case would be tried first, on a change of venue to Lubbock County.

The trial began on Monday, February 5, 1935, in Lubbock's stately 1916 courthouse. Described as "calm, cocky and pudgy-faced," Stalcup smoked constantly during the proceedings. With his blonde wife holding his hand, Stalcup's five-year-old daughter clambered over his lap, kissing him repeatedly as two dozen officers stood nearby for security.

Stalcup's young court-appointed lawyers were from Lubbock: Hugh Anderson, Dub Benson and Robert Allen. The prosecution was led by special prosecutor George Dupree, a legendary Lubbock trial lawyer. Dickens County DA Alton Chapman and Lubbock County DA Dan Blair augmented the state's team. They subpoenaed sixty witnesses.

The 1909 Dickens County Jail, where Sheriff Bill Arthur was murdered in 1934. *Courtesy of Dickens County.*

Jury selection was completed on Tuesday, and when testimony began on Wednesday morning, the courtroom was packed with observers. Another two hundred were turned away.

The state's first three witnesses were prisoners present in the jail when Sheriff Arthur was murdered, but none saw the attack. Jenks Yarbrough, serving a fifteen-year prison sentence for a previous shooting of the sheriff, testified that he looked up when he heard the shot and saw Stalcup "holding a big gun."

Inmates Curtis Squyres and Luther Hall both saw Stalcup with a "drawn pistol" after the shot rang out. Squyres hollered for help as Stalcup ran down the stairs. Stalcup yelled, "Shut your [expletive] mouth." Hall saw Stalcup open the cellblock door with keys in his left hand and saw Brown follow Stalcup down the stairs.

The sheriff's twelve-year-old daughter, Creola, was home in her family's first-floor jail apartment when she heard the shot. Tearfully, Creola told the jury she saw the jail door open and Stalcup with a gun. As Stalcup drove away in the sheriff's car, Creola chased on foot, returning to see her daddy's lifeless body being carried down the stairs.

Stalcup never testified but granted interviews to a reporter during the trial. "I didn't kill the man," he said, refusing to name the shooter. He praised Sheriff Arthur. "I admired him myself. I respected him. He was always kind to me."

A firearms expert testified the gun used to kill the sheriff could not have been either of the two weapons known to belong to the sheriff, a .38 and a .45. An older model revolver was presented as evidence. It had been left at Brown's brother-in-law's home by Stalcup and Brown after their jailbreak. However, no evidence was offered to show that Brown's wife smuggled the revolver into the jail, and no evidence connected the revolver to the sheriff's murder.

The state rested. The defense called a dozen quick but ineffective witnesses, most of whom had already testified for the state. Impassioned final arguments lasted six hours on Monday, February 11, and jury deliberations began. The unanimous guilty verdict came at 9:13 Tuesday morning, and the jury recommended the death sentence.

A slight twitching of the lips was the only emotion Stalcup displayed during the entire trial, but it did not last long. Two minutes after the verdict, the condemned man was smiling as he shook hands with his lawyer.

In April 1935, a slender and bespectacled Clarence Brown pled guilty to the sheriff's murder and was sentenced to ninety-nine years in prison. He died in the Texas State Penitentiary in 1959. His wife, Thelma, was sentenced to two years in prison for smuggling the pistol into the jail. She served thirteen months in the pen and seemed to disappear.

A year later, Stalcup's appeals failed. He was returned from death row to Lubbock to receive his execution date. He spoke to reporters, who wrote that he had "lost his bravado and embraced the Catholic faith." Again, he denied killing the sheriff and complained of "perjured testimony" during his trial. "There's a higher power that will even up all these things some time. They'll have to pay for it someday."

His execution date was scheduled for May 4, 1936. Stalcup left the courtroom arm-in-arm with his mother, but his wife and daughter were not present. During a search, authorities found that he was in possession of Sheriff Arthur's handcuff key, though it did not fit the shackles he was wearing.

The evening before he was to be electrocuted, Stalcup was offered a special last meal. He refused. At 12:03 a.m., he walked firmly to "Old Sparky" and died calmly without making a statement.

10

HISTORY OF LUBBOCK COUNTY EXECUTIONS

Hundreds of murder trials have been staged in Lubbock County. Some resulted in acquittals or mistrials, and many ended in convictions. But only a few of those convicted of murder were executed for their crimes.

Lubbock's first murder trial, in 1913, was *State v. William E. Taylor*, for the murder of Tom Collins. Taylor, a deputy city marshal, shot and killed Collins and J.J. Reynolds at the Blue Front Restaurant. His self-defense claim was successful, and the second case against Taylor, for killing Reynolds, was dismissed.

Twenty years later, the first death sentence was handed down by a Lubbock County jury. Paul Mitchell was convicted of killing Robert Tharp during the 1932 armed robbery of a grocery store. The *Lubbock Avalanche-Journal* reported Mitchell's response to the jury's 1933 verdict: "It hit me kind of hard, but I can stand the gaff." In 1934, his death warrant was commuted to a life sentence by Governor Ma Ferguson. Then, in 1950, Mitchell was granted a full pardon by Governor Allan Shivers.

In 1934, a Dickens County case was transferred to Lubbock for the trial of Virgil Stalcup. Stalcup was convicted of murdering Dickens County sheriff W.B. Arthur during a jailbreak. He was electrocuted at Huntsville in 1936, becoming the first defendant tried in Lubbock County and executed.

The first Lubbock County crime resulting in an execution was *State v. Walter E. Whitaker Jr.* The twenty-year-old Reese Air Force Base airman was tried for the January 1953 strangulation of his eighteen-year-old girlfriend, Joyce Fern White. His fate was decided six months later by a Wilbarger County jury on a change of venue. Whitaker was electrocuted on September 1, 1954.

No other Lubbock County defendant died in "Old Sparky," Huntsville's electric chair and Texas' official execution method from 1924 to 1964. Before 1924, Texas executions were conducted locally in the county of conviction—usually by public hanging—and there is no record of a Lubbock County hanging or other form of execution prior to Whitaker's electrocution.

Between 1967 and 1977, the U.S. death penalty was suspended. Since its reinstatement, eight Lubbock County defendants have been executed by lethal injection.

Michael McBride was convicted of the 1985 shooting deaths of his ex-girlfriend, Christian Fisher, and her companion, James Alan Holzer, outside McBride's home. Fisher went to the house to collect some personal items, and McBride confronted her with a rifle. He shot Fisher, walked to the car and shot Holzer, then shot himself in the head, but he survived. McBride was executed on May 11, 2000.

Cecil Joiner was convicted in the 1986 stabbing deaths of two waitresses, Carol Lynette Huckabee, twenty-six, and Eva Marie DeForest, twenty-nine. Both were bound with duct tape and stabbed repeatedly. Joiner lived next door. Bloodstains found on Joiner's shirt tested positive for both women's blood types. His execution was on July 12, 2000.

Mack Hill was convicted in the 1987 robbery-murder of his sometime business partner, Donald Franklin Johnson. Johnson's body was found five months after his disappearance in a fifty-five-gallon drum that had been filled with concrete and dumped into a lake. After Johnson's disappearance, Hill was seen with Johnson's pickup and camper trailer. He was implicated in the theft of items from Johnson's paint and body shop and the sale of those items at local flea markets. Hill was lethally injected on August 8, 2001.

Adolph Hernandez was convicted in the 1988 robbery and murder of sixty-nine-year-old Elizabeth Alvarado in Slaton. Hernandez beat her to death with a baseball bat in her home. The victim's daughter confronted Hernandez, wrestled the bat from him and hit him with it. He was arrested with bloodstains on his shirt, pants and shoes. His execution was on February 8, 2001.

In October 1989, Jack Clark murdered twenty-three-year-old Melisa Ann Garcia of Slaton. She suffered two fatal stab wounds to the chest after she was abducted, forced into Clark's car, taken to a remote area and sexually assaulted. He died by lethal injection on January 9, 2001.

Robert Salazar Jr. fatally injured a two-year-old girl, Adriana Gomez, in 1997. He was babysitting the victim. Salazar inflicted wounds consisting of a fractured skull, bruised heart, fractured ribs and ruptured intestines. After injuring the girl, Salazar placed her in her crib and left the residence. The girl's mother arrived home from work, finding her in her crib and noting that Salazar was absent. Adriana was pronounced dead at a hospital. Salazar's execution took place on March 22, 2006.

In 1997, Michael Rosales burglarized the home of sixty-eight-year-old Mary Felder, who surprised him during the burglary. He stabbed her 137 times with a kitchen knife and struck her on the head with a hard object. Rosales was executed on April 15, 2009.

Rosendo Rodriguez III, known as the "Suitcase Murderer," was convicted of the September 2005 rape and murder of twenty-nine-year-old Summer Baldwin in Lubbock. Her body was found in a suitcase in a Lubbock landfill. Rodriguez had purchased the suitcase. He was executed on March 27, 2018.

Two convicted Lubbock County murderers remain on death row: Brian Suniga and Joe Franco Garza.

11

THE LAW ACCORDING
TO CHAPPELL

H is more celebrated contemporaries—Travis Shelton, George Gilkerson, Clifford Brown—are considered icons of the Texas criminal bar. But Byron Chappell 's low-key, practical, yet zealous and imaginative approach to his craft has inspired Lubbock lawyers for decades.

Chappell was born in Midland in 1916. After obtaining undergraduate and graduate degrees at Texas Tech, he taught school at Lubbock's Guadalupe Elementary and Carroll Thompson Junior High Schools. His experience teaching minority kids in these low-income neighborhoods was a positive influence on his later career representing Black and Hispanic clients.

When World War II erupted, Chappell became a bomber navigator in the U.S. Army Air Corps. His war stories were vibrant but vague, downplaying his heroics while casting himself as a sort of Milo from the novel *Catch-22*, supplying cigarettes, chocolates, nylons and other contraband to fellow servicemen.

After the war, Chappell worked as a shoe salesman in Austin to finance his study of law at the University of Texas. He learned to accurately assess anyone's shoe size with just a glance, a skill he would one day put to use in the courtroom.

He returned to Lubbock after passing the bar exam in 1948, joining his father, Bell Chappell, and Roy Carpenter in the practice of law. Soon, his father died and Carpenter left the firm, but Byron acquired Carpenter's six-carat diamond ring, which Byron wore until his death. He was proud to flash Carpenter's huge rock, amused when his clients bragged, "My lawyer has a bigger diamond than your lawyer!"

Friday was payday for Chappell's working-class clients, who often blew their entire weekly wage before Monday. So, on Friday evenings, Chappell boldly drove his pink Chrysler Imperial convertible through East Lubbock, the Guadalupe community, the "Flats" and Slaton's shadiest neighborhoods, sometimes accompanied by his blonde bombshell wife, Rosalie. His clients easily recognized the flashy convertible and ran out to greet their lawyer. After attorney fee obligations were resolved, Chappell would be on his way.

Byron "Lawyer" Chappell late in his career. *Photo by Chuck Lanehart.*

It may seem amazing that his giant diamond ring was never stolen on Chappell's rounds through these tough environs, but his clients loved him and protected him.

Many stories involve the Lawyer Chappell method of making money. Late one night, Chappell was called to spring a fellow from jail who promised he had cash money. Alas, once the client was sprung, all he had of value were the ostrich-skin boots on his feet. Chappell took the boots and sent him away barefoot. The next morning, the client appeared at Chappell's office with cash, and the boots were returned.

The day before a negotiated plea of guilty, clients would appear in Chappell's office to prepare for the court appearance. Sometimes, the client owed a balance on Chappell's attorney fee. On those occasions, Chappell would tell the client, "The first question that judge will ask you tomorrow will be, 'Have you paid your lawyer in full?'" (No judge ever asked such a question.) If all else failed, Chappell forgave the balance due. The charitable gesture encouraged clients to return and refer others. He also represented many indigent clients *pro bono*.

Chappell, famous for his talent collecting fees, also had a talent for setting fees. His philosophy was to charge whatever the traffic would bear. "You quote the biggest fee you think the client can pay," he advised. "Watch the client carefully. If he gasps at your quote, you can negotiate. On the other hand, if the client reaches for his wallet, just say, 'That will be the down payment.'"

"Many folks accused of crimes are guilty of something, but they are usually over-accused by some stupid prosecutor," Chappell said. "They're looking for a fair deal, and they want a lawyer who will fight hard for the best deal available. If you fight hard, you will satisfy your clients. Get the client to pay a fee that will justify your efforts in fighting hard for your client, and you will be successful."

As a trial lawyer, Chappell won some and lost some, but he always gave his best effort. He rarely handled high-profile cases, and he never sought the spotlight.

In 1963, however, Chappell's face flickered across TV screens, and his name made the front page of the *Lubbock Avalanche-Journal*. His paralegal, Marcos Hernandez, was acting as an interpreter for another lawyer's client in a DWI trial. District Attorney George Gilkerson objected, claiming that Hernandez had a conflict because he worked for a "bail bond lawyer." Chappell, a spectator in the gallery, stood and objected to Gilkerson's objection. An outraged Gilkerson charged Chappell, catching him with a left to the chin. Chappell hit the floor, and the incident soon resulted in Gilkerson leaving the DA's office. After the infamous punch, Lawyer Chappell's advice to young attorneys was, "Carry a heavy clipboard to the courthouse for self-defense."

In the mid-1970s, a Lubbock convenience store was robbed by a young African American man. The police found a pair of gaudy yellow patent-leather platform shoes the culprit had lost while running from the scene. The police detective got a tip that the shoes belonged to Byron "Lawyer" Chappell's client, and the man was arrested.

At trial, the detective—known for his racially insensitive views—testified that the shoes fit Chappell's client. On cross-examination, the lawyer proposed that the shoes might fit many people in the community, but the detective disagreed. Chappell—the former shoe salesman—reached into his pocket, produced a shoehorn, grabbed the shoes and asked the detective to try them on.

After vigorous objections from the prosecutor, the judge allowed the demonstration. The detective's face turned red. He began to sweat and wiggle in the witness chair as Chappell approached with the offensive shoes and shoehorn, confident he had calculated the detective's exact shoe size. Sure enough, the shoes fit the detective perfectly.

Unfortunately, other evidence convinced the jury to find the client guilty, but Chappell arranged a reasonable punishment. His shoe stunt—which publicly embarrassed the racist detective—became legendary in the minority community and beyond.

Chappell represented a young man named Milton Morales, who one day wandered into a convenience store shopping for sunglasses. The clerk called the cops and told them Milton had robbed her a couple of weeks earlier. He was arrested and went to trial.

Chappell cross-examined the clerk.

> *Q: You are positive Milton is the person who robbed you?*
> *A: Yes.*
> *Q: He robbed you and ran out of the store?*
> *A: Yes.*
> *Q: He ran out real fast, about as fast as you have seen anyone run?*
> *A: Yes.*
> *Q: You didn't notice anything unusual about the way he ran out of the store?*
> *A: No.*

Chappell turned to his client. "Milton, run as fast as you can to the back wall of the courtroom." Before the prosecutor could catch his breath, Milton began limping as quickly as he could manage. It was painful to watch, because Milton had been afflicted with polio as a child. One of his thighs was about the size of a baseball bat.

The jury quickly acquitted Milton. The case didn't make the papers, but Chappell's people knew he had put another notch in his lawyer belt.

Chappell's manner of speech was a curious blend of colorful colloquialisms, archaic adages and vulgarity. The following is a sanitized glossary of "Chappellisms":

"This is where we're sittin'." Chappell's prelude to telling a client the unvarnished truth.

"I need to feel the bumps on his head." To convey a plea offer to a client.

"I'll be happy to sit next to you during your trial." Discouraging words to a client slow to pay his trial fee.

"Crazy as a peach orchard bore." Description of any client who failed to follow Chappell's advice.

"He squealed like a pig under a gate." Client's reaction to an unreasonable plea offer.

"Fifty years ain't long if you say it real fast." Sarcastic response to a prosecutor's unreasonable plea offer.

"Meaner than bar whiskey." Description of a worthy opponent.

"Two-bit politician." Description of elected DAs or judges who failed to understand Chappell's wisdom.

"Thanks for the use of your courtroom." Spoken with tongue in cheek to an unhelpful judge following a jury acquittal.

"He doesn't know s——t from Shinola." Description of an unhelpful judge.

"But he's got a good mama." Used in plea negotiations with prosecutors. Some clients had few admirable attributes.

"Pup." Young associate lawyer.

"I like her. She's a spender." Description of a pup's wife. High-maintenance spouses were an incentive for pups to work harder.

"Don't tell me I can't do that!" Chappell's response to a pup's adverse legal research.

"You learnin' anything?" Meant to encourage underpaid pups, in order to justify small salaries.

"You hired out to work when you left the farm!" Advice to pups who complained of heavy workloads.

"You better back up to that paycheck!" When pups failed to match expectations.

"Don't let them rot in jail." It is impossible to render effective assistance to a jailed client.

"All I got was his damn squawk box!" Chappell hated voice mail and answering machines, which were never implemented in his office.

"Make friends with your opponent. Then fight hard. The scars will be less likely to last." Common Chappell advice.

"Always satisfy your client." Chappell's most common advice.

"It will all work out." Chappell's motto.

In 1989, Chappell was the first person inducted into the Lubbock Criminal Defense Lawyers Hall of Fame. He was bestowed the Lubbock County Bar Association's highest honor, the James G. Denton Distinguished Lawyer Award, posthumously in 2000. Lawyer Chappell practiced until shortly before his death in 2000 at age eighty-three.

12

THE LAWSUIT THAT WON DIVERSITY IN LUBBOCK LEADERSHIP

Jones v. the City

When Gene Gaines' wife died in the 1970s, he was told she must be buried in the segregated Black/Mexican American section of the City of Lubbock Cemetery. Offended by the city's racial discrimination, Gaines—Lubbock's first Black lawyer—decided to take legal action to desegregate the all-Anglo Lubbock City Council, which was charged with cemetery policy.

Newsman Skip Watson covered the lawsuit and remembered, "The story of this litigation began as a blemish that grew into a boil, which ultimately had to be taken to the Appellate Court of the United States to be lanced."

After the City of Lubbock was incorporated in 1909, the city charter of 1917 systematically excluded Black people and Mexican Americans from elected leadership positions for the next six-plus decades. The controversy was addressed in a bitterly litigated eight-year federal lawsuit.

In Lubbock's "at large" system, voters throughout the city elected council and mayoral candidates, and it mattered not in which part of the city the candidate resided. At the time of the lawsuit, Lubbock's population was approximately 74 percent Anglo, 18 percent Mexican American and 8 percent Black. Minorities, who lived primarily in north and east neighborhoods of the city, had never fielded a successful candidate for mayor or city council.

A minority candidate could be quite talented, invest money, run a big campaign and even have support among Anglos, but ultimately, when the returns came in, the Anglo majority would vote for Anglo candidates, and Anglos always won.

U.S. district judge Halbert O. Woodward presided over *Jones v. City of Lubbock* between 1976 and 1984. *Author's collection.*

In 1976, Gaines filed a class-action lawsuit in Judge Halbert O. Woodward's Lubbock federal court to require the city to abandon its at-large election system.

Gaines had little experience in federal civil rights litigation, so Texas Tech law professor Dan Benson volunteered to substitute as lead counsel, and Gaines became a witness in the case rather than an advocate.

Benson, forty, was a Lubbock native and grandson of W.D. Benson, a prominent pioneer lawyer who arrived in Lubbock in 1902. Benson recruited several young Lubbock lawyers to assist, including Lane and Nancy Arthur, Tomás Garza, Mark C. Hall and Albert Perez. All agreed to work pro bono. Collectively, they represented the minority plaintiffs: the Reverend Roy Jones, Gonzalo Garza, Eusebio Morales and Rose Wilson.

The plaintiffs' amended petition alleged that the election scheme not only resulted in minority electoral defeats but also effectively denied Lubbock's Black and Mexican American voters equal access to the political process.

The Lubbock City Council voted to defend the 1917 city charter's at-large electoral system. Members were fearful that single-member districts would result in a "ward system" similar to that of Chicago, creating corruption and a racially divisive political climate in Lubbock.

The city's defense team was headed by powerful former Lubbock County district attorney Travis Shelton, president of the State Bar of Texas (1977–78) and member of the Texas Criminal Defense Lawyers Association's Hall of Fame. Shelton was joined by his firm's associates, Dennis McGill and Dale Jones, along with City Attorney John Ross of Lubbock and his assistant, James Brewster.

Sentiments ran hot on both sides of the controversy. Benson said there was even an effort to get him fired from his professorship at the Tech law school.

Mark C. Hall remembered, "At trial, we had to open up a whole lot of old wounds that had been healing over time," and evidence of Lubbock's shameful racist history was produced.

Between 1909 and 1924, editorials in the *Lubbock Avalanche* appeared on subjects ranging from the Black electoral franchise to the very presence of Black people in the city. The editorials contained a series of vile racial slurs at a time when fewer than seventy Black people populated Lubbock. Editorials said "Negroes" would carry disease, cause crime and invite further influx of Negroes into Lubbock. An editorial in 1909 recommended disenfranchising Black people; another in 1924 warned of Black efforts to exert political influence. The author of the offensive articles, *Avalanche* editor James Dow, was a member of the 1917 city charter commission.

A 1923 city ordinance made it a crime for "Negroes" to live in any part of Lubbock other than areas designated in East Lubbock.

Charles Guy, former editor of the *Lubbock Avalanche-Journal*, testified for the plaintiffs. Describing the considerable history of Ku Klux Klan influence in the city, Guy believed each of the 1917 city charter commissioners were KKK members. An expert witness testified that exclusion of participation by minorities—both racial and political—provided a partial motive for the movement to at-large government.

In 1979, Judge Woodward ruled against the plaintiffs, who appealed to the Fifth Circuit Court of Appeals in New Orleans. While the appeal was pending, the United States Supreme Court handed down a number of dramatic decisions supporting the plaintiff's position, and Congress amended the Voting Rights Act, which also supported the plaintiffs' position. The case was therefore remanded for a new trial.

In the 1983 second trial, the plaintiffs had the law on their side and relied extensively on the evidence produced in the 1979 trial. Judge Woodward found the City of Lubbock's at-large scheme violated both the Fifteenth Amendment and Section 2 of the Voting Rights Act. He found that the system had discriminatory results and that the motives of the original charter committee that adopted the at-large system had been "invidious."

Judge Woodward ordered a new plan for city elections, which called for a six-member council elected from single-member districts and a mayor elected at-large. The plan retained both the prior terms of office and staggered terms for council members.

The city's appeal to the Fifth Circuit failed. The Fifth Circuit's opinion found:

> *No minority candidate is ever likely to serve on an at-large city council. Neither Black nor Mexican American voters, whether voting separately or as a coalition, are ever likely to elect a candidate of their choice in*

Lubbock without substantial Anglo support. Lubbock's voting preferences, however, are clear; whatever other characteristics the candidate of minority choice may have, that candidate will face a serious obstacle to obtaining substantial Anglo support if he or she is Black or Mexican American. In short, we do not doubt that the system will allow a bloc voting majority over a substantial period of time consistently to defeat minority candidates.

Part of Judge Woodward's ruling was overturned, but the Fifth Circuit's 1984 decision was a huge victory for the plaintiffs. The editors of the *Lubbock Avalanche-Journal* and many other powerful members of the community were outraged by the decision. They pushed for an appeal to the U.S. Supreme Court in defense of the city's at-large voting system.

An *AJ* editorial claimed: "The people are being denied their constitutional right to decide how to elect councilmen; the courts are dictating to them. Absent a vote of the people to change the city charter, the council has a certain legal obligation to defend them against a judicial usurpation of power so long as any hope exists of ultimate victory."

The city council sought a stay from the Fifth Circuit, but the council soon realized that single-member districts were an inevitable reality and backed off. Mayor Alan Henry made the formal announcement of the council's acceptance of the ruling, proclaiming, "Minority citizens will not just be supplicants and petitioners but office holders."

Soon, Lubbock's first two minority members of the city council were elected: Maggie Trejo and T.J. Patterson. Trejo, a 1979 graduate of Texas Tech, had been administrative assistant for Texas District 83 representative Froy Salinas. She knew the importance of finding an effective voice for her community.

Patterson, a longtime civil rights activist and editor of the *Southwest Digest*, was approached by a prominent local businessman who warned, "T.J., I will be watching you." He ignored the veiled threat and maintained his dignity when he ventured into southwest Lubbock on official city business, faced with racially-charged situations.

T.J. Patterson, the first Black member of the Lubbock City Council. *Courtesy of City of Lubbock.*

In 2014, T.J. recalled, "There were two of us, Maggie and me, and when we voted nay, they couldn't get nothing through. We had some muscle with that. In a lot of things you do, you learn by doing. And it paid off for the benefit and the welfare of Lubbock."

Mayor Henry said, "I think that T.J. and Maggie were placed on this Earth to be in those two council seats. I really, truly believe that. We had heard horror stories, from some of the cities in Texas, and some of the problems that they had, as far as not being able to get along, not being able to talk to each other, and what I thought—territorialism—to the point that each council member said, 'The rest of you all stay out. This is my turf. This is my district.' And it makes it very, very difficult to look at the picture."

Plaintiff's attorney Mark Hall remembered, "I'm proud to live in Lubbock, to have been born and raised here. I felt so strongly about this case. I am so thankful for being here and able to help on the case. It's real important that this community has stayed together all this time. Everybody's had their political differences, but it has stayed together."

There is disagreement about whether Lubbock's 1984 single-member district change had much of an effect. Floyd Price, who replaced Patterson as District 2 representative in 2004, noted that minority leaders on the council have only come from Districts 1 and 2 and a nonwhite mayor has yet to be elected.

"Nothing's changed," Price said. "What America was built on was diversity and, so in order to really grow as a city, as a state, as a nation, you have to have diversity. And, if you have the same old thing all the time, how much change do you get?"

13

DID JACK BROWN
KILL HIS PARENTS?

The Circumstantial Shallowater Murder Case

Everyone assumed Dolphus Jack Brown murdered his parents at their Shallowater farmhouse in the spring of 1967. Jack certainly had the opportunity, and perhaps a motive, but the evidence against him was circumstantial. Forensic evidence of the era was unimpressive, and no DNA science or video surveillance existed that might have clearly exonerated or condemned Jack. The high-profile case pitted giants of the Lubbock bar against one another.

D.J. "Buzz" Brown was a prominent insurance agent and farmer west of Lubbock. He and his wife, Birdie, lived near Shallowater with their only child, Jack, age twenty-five. The Browns were admired in their community and were considered wealthy. Jack was good-looking and popular, salutatorian and male favorite of his 1960 graduating class at Shallowater High School. After graduation, he served in the military and later enrolled at Texas Tech.

In the early morning hours of April 18, 1967, Jack summoned sheriff's deputies to the family home. He said he found the bloody bodies of Buzz and Birdie inside the home after he returned from a poker game about 3:00 a.m. Jack's parents were found in their nightclothes in their bedroom. Both had been beaten about their heads with an unknown blunt object, and they had died of brain trauma.

The autopsy report estimated the time of death at 2:00 a.m., but definitely between 12:00 a.m. and 4:00 a.m. No murder weapon was identified. There was no evidence of forced entry, of an intruder or of robbery. Jack's shirt with tiny spots of blood was found in the laundry hamper.

At noon, Jack voluntarily submitted to an interview with Lubbock County district attorney Alton Griffin and investigators. He appeared without counsel and freely discussed his whereabouts the previous night. He had an alibi. He denied any knowledge of blood spots on the shirt. When asked if he had changed any other apparel, he slapped his leg and said, "No, these are the same pants I had on all day yesterday."

Jack said he was shacked up at a Lubbock motel with a girl, Anita Roberson, most of the afternoon and evening of April 17. Sometime before 7:30 p.m., he drove home and changed shirts, telling his parents he intended to play poker that night. He played poker with friends at a Lubbock home until about 2:00 a.m. with the exception of a break of one hour, when he returned to the motel for a sandwich with Anita. He checked out of the motel at 3:00 a.m. and drove home to find his parents dead.

Jack's innocent activities that night—covering the time period the forensic pathologist said his parents died—seemed strange, but multiple witnesses corroborated his whereabouts.

About the same time Jack was being questioned, evidence was discovered in a dumpster in Lubbock's Mackenzie State Park, about twenty minutes from the murder scene. Bloody clothes the Browns were wearing earlier on April 17 were found cut down the back. A wet, bloody towel bearing Jack's army serial number and a pair of bloody trousers were also found in the dumpster.

There were no eyewitness, no murder weapon, no forensic evidence and no confession connecting Jack to the murders, but within twelve hours of Jack finding the bodies of his parents, he was charged with "murder with malice," a capital crime. He was jailed without bail. For District Attorney Griffin, known as a fearless bulldog of a prosecutor, the case was a challenge he relished.

Lined up against Griffin were two former Lubbock County DAs, George Gilkerson and Travis Shelton, formidable opponents who would later be inducted into multiple legal halls of fame.

Meanwhile, on May 11, 1967, Gilkerson and Shelton, on Jack's behalf, filed an application to probate the wills of Buzz and Birdie, who left their estate—thought to be substantial—to Jack.

Pretrial matters dragged on for more than a year. Lubbock County district judge James A. Ellis finally released Jack on $25,000 bail. The case dominated the news, and the defense argued that Jack could not get a fair trial in Lubbock. Judge Ellis agreed and transferred the case to El Paso's Thirty-Fourth District Court on a change of venue.

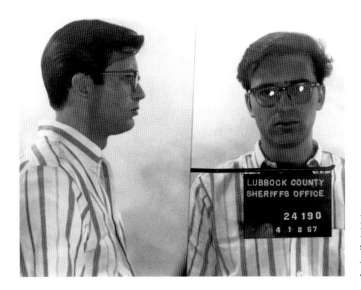

Dolphus Jack Brown mug shot. *Courtesy of Lubbock County Sheriff's Office.*

But El Paso was inhospitable to the defense. The new judge, William E. Ward, swiftly turned down every pretrial motion offered by Gilkerson and Shelton.

Jack got lucky when DA Griffin decided not to seek the death penalty. Griffin's decision was influenced by a national de facto moratorium on the death penalty as litigation challenging insidious capital punishment laws worked its way through the courts in the late 1960s. In 1972, the U.S. Supreme Court struck down Georgia's capital crime laws, resulting in a restructuring of death penalty statutes nationwide.

Jack, now facing a maximum punishment of life imprisonment rather than the electric chair, appeared for trial in El Paso on October 8, 1968. Following jury selection, Jack Brown faced an all-male jury in El Paso and pled "not guilty." Judge William E. Ward sequestered the jury. About fifty witnesses, including thirty-four for the state, were expected to testify.

Before the jury heard evidence, the prosecution called detectives to respond to the defense's allegation of an illegal search of the Brown home. Judge Ward denied the motion to suppress evidence and denied a defense motion for continuance based on newly discovered evidence. Jack, wearing a gray suit, showed signs of strain for the first time in all of his court appearances.

When testimony began on October 11, Jack silently wept, dabbing his red, wet eyes with a handkerchief as a pathologist described horrific injuries to his parents, Buzz and Birdie Brown, bludgeoned to death on April 18, 1967, in their Shallowater home.

In a surprising turn of events, the pathologist changed his opinion as to the time of their deaths. He originally reported the couple died between 12:00 a.m. and 4:00 a.m., when witnesses swore Jack was with his girlfriend and at a poker game. He instead told the jury: "I really don't know what time they died. It could have been several hours before," a period when Jack's whereabouts was not so clear.

Items found in a dumpster in Mackenzie State Park were introduced: personal items belonging to Buzz and a pair of bloody coveralls he wore the evening of April 17. Birdie's bloody gray-and-white-checked dress she wore the same evening was offered in evidence, as was a bloody towel connected to Jack's military service. A pair of bloodstained men's slacks found in the dumpster was also admitted into evidence.

The dumpster items were evaluated for blood type, which matched Buzz's type O and Birdie's type A, but the analysis failed to incriminate Jack. However, the girl Jack entertained in a Lubbock motel that evening identified the bloody slacks and a shirt stained with drops of blood found in a laundry hamper at the Brown house as "what the defendant was wearing."

Griffin proposed that Jack murdered his parents before 8:00 p.m., played poker with friends, returned home later in the evening, cut the Browns' clothing from them, dressed them for bed, changed his clothing, left the residence, hid the bloody evidence and returned home about 3:30 a.m. to "discover" the bodies.

The DA also presented evidence of motive—greed—for the murders: a former girlfriend testified that she loaned Jack $200 and he did not repay the debt. The evidence of greed seemed weak, though it was true that Jack stood to inherit from his parents the equivalent of more than $1 million in today's terms. The jury did not hear the inheritance evidence.

Gilkerson and Shelton presented an alibi defense, as a parade of witnesses documented his whereabouts the evening of April 7 and the early morning of April 8. A pathologist called by the defense testified that the state's autopsy findings were "logically impossible" and estimated the Browns died between 1:00 a.m. and 3:00 a.m., when Jack's strongest alibi witnesses supported his presence elsewhere.

The jury deliberated less than six hours on October 16 before returning a verdict of guilty. As the punishment phase of the trial began, Jack looked pale and worried. Defense witnesses described his good character. Lubbock physician John Chalk, with whom Jack had lived after making bail, said Jack was "one of the kindest and gentlest persons I've ever been around," practically a member of the family.

Following spirited final arguments, the jury decided Jack should spend thirteen years in prison for murdering his parents. It seemed a lenient sentence for a guilty man, but Jack maintained his innocence. He remained free on appeal bonds as Gilkerson and Shelton spent years litigating appeals, to no avail.

Meanwhile, no one objected to Jack's application to probate his parents' wills. After all debts were paid, he collected about $21,000 ($150,000 in 2022 dollars) from their estates.

In March 1972, Jack became a prison inmate at the Wynn Unit, Huntsville. He served only five years of his thirteen-year sentence before being released on parole on May 12, 1977, just over ten years following the death of his parents.

Jack married and raised a family, living and working in several Texas towns, but he never again saw Shallowater. In 2012, at age seventy, he died from injuries sustained in an auto accident and was buried in LaRue, Henderson County, survived by his widow, five children and nine grandchildren.

14

AMARILLO AND THE CASE OF CULLEN DAVIS, THE RICHEST MAN TRIED FOR MURDER

Amarillo was the site of one of the most notable trials of the twentieth century, a case that combined sex, violence and immense wealth with flamboyant legal maneuvers and saturation publicity. Amarillo jurors sat through the longest criminal trial in Texas history; listened to the most witnesses to testify in a criminal prosecution in Texas history; and decided the fate of the richest man ever tried for murder in American history.

Born in 1933, Cullen Davis was the son of legendary Fort Worth oilman "Stinky" Davis. After Stinky's death in 1968, Cullen inherited a fortune worth $750 million in today's dollars.

Within days of his father's death, Cullen married twenty-six-year-old Priscilla Lee Childers, a flashy, petite blonde from the small Texas town of Dublin. She had three children from prior relationships, including Andrea Wilborn, born in 1964. Cullen insisted Priscilla transform herself into a sex symbol, with dyed platinum hair, huge breast implants and the skimpiest of glitzy gowns and bikinis. He also insisted she sign a prenuptial agreement.

The couple launched an ostentatious spending spree: a Learjet, world travel, jewelry, art and a multimillion-dollar home on Fort Worth's Mockingbird Lane known as Stonegate Mansion.

By 1974, the marriage was on the rocks. As both spouses dated others, the divorce judge granted Priscilla the right to live in Stonegate and ordered Cullen to make substantial support payments. Cullen was furious with the ruling.

On the night of August 2, 1976, an ambulance was dispatched to the mansion. The driver spotted a blond, bosomy woman limping across the lawn. It was Priscilla.

"What happened?" he asked as he jumped out of the vehicle.

"I've been shot!"

"Who shot you?"

"My husband!"

"Who is your husband?"

"Cullen Davis."

Meanwhile, eighteen-year-old Beverly Bass and her boyfriend, Bubba Gavrel, arrived at the mansion. They were confronted by the gunman, who shot Bubba, paralyzing him for life. Beverly, a family friend, told police that Cullen was the shooter. "I've known him since I was a little girl."

Inside the mansion, investigators discovered a bloody, horrific scene. Priscilla's twelve-year-old daughter, Andrea Wilborn, was found shot dead in the basement. Priscilla's live-in boyfriend, Stan Farr, was also dead.

Police questioned Cullen. "What would be a good enough reason for two people ending up getting killed like this?" a detective asked.

Cullen looked directly at the detective. "Sometimes, a man doesn't need a reason."

He was arrested for two murders and two attempted murders. Less than twenty-four hours later, Cullen posted an $80,000 cash bond and was released. Publicity in the Metroplex was intense. Tarrant County district attorney Tim Curry came under pressure to upgrade the charge to capital murder, which would empower the court to deny bond.

As Cullen—reportedly bound for Venezuela—approached the door to his Learjet, he was arrested for the capital murders of Stan Farr and Andrea Wilborn. Bond was denied.

He hired the best attorneys money could buy, including powerful Dallas lawyer Phil Burleson. For lead counsel, Cullen chose Richard "Racehorse" Haynes of Houston, master of winning impossible cases. Haynes, forty-seven, was short, barrel-chested, big-headed and bow-legged. He wore the most expensive suits and cowboy boots, and by 1974, no one doubted his claim to be one of the best criminal defense lawyers in Texas. "If Nixon had hired me," he boasted, "he would still be president."

Cullen's lawyers immediately filed motions to release him on bond. At the bond hearing, DA Curry produced wheelchair-bound witnesses and shocking revelations about Cullen's history of brutality toward women, children and small animals. It was a public-relations victory for the prosecution. It

Stan Farr and Priscilla Davis, circa 1976. *Courtesy of NBC 5KXAS Photograph Collection AR0847, University of North Texas Special Collections.*

hardened the public's heart against "the millionaire who thought he could get away with murder." Cullen would remain incarcerated through his trial.

The over-the-top publicity meant a fair jury could not be found in Fort Worth, so a change of venue was granted to Amarillo, 340 miles to the northwest. It was an isolated Panhandle city of less than 145,000 people. The new judge would be George Dowlen, a toothpick-chewing good ol' boy known as honorable, fair and gentlemanly.

Jury selection took place in the summer of 1977, and when the dust settled, nine men and three women between the ages of twenty-six and sixty-four were seated. Most were working people. The prosecution thought they'd be fair. The defense thought they'd hate Priscilla because of her flash and sordid lifestyle.

When Priscilla Davis arrived in Amarillo, she and her entourage landed in a baby-blue jet and were whisked off in a limousine to the Presidential Suite at the Amarillo Hilton. Dressed in a white dress with ruffles, Priscilla wore a gold cross around her neck and carried a white, leatherbound Bible.

Cullen, the quiet, slim, handsome millionaire, seemed like a movie star to many in Amarillo.

Haynes was determined to put Priscilla on trial, not his client, Cullen Davis.

The setting for the most anticipated trial in Texas history was a nondescript courtroom in Amarillo, and the outcome of the double-murder case hinged on the testimony of multimillionaire defendant Cullen Davis' estranged wife, Priscilla Davis. Each of the fifty-two gallery seats was filled, and ten lawyers crowded around the big counsel table.

Forensic evidence offered from the medical examiner was subjected to seven excruciating days of cross-examination by defense lawyer Haynes, until jurors were convinced scientific testimony could be ignored.

Next came Priscilla, one of two eyewitnesses who identified Cullen as the shooter. She appeared each day in a different new Neiman Marcus dress, accented by her big, bright platinum hair. It was not an Amarillo look. The defense knew what the jurors were thinking: Priscilla was a girl from the wrong side of the tracks who would do or say anything not to go home to her past.

Haynes questioned Priscilla for days, relentlessly building on the defense contention that she and the other eyewitness, Beverly Bass, had concocted their story to keep the real killer from coming after them and to help Priscilla get Cullen's millions in the divorce. "I know I'm not Miss Goody Two-shoes," she told reporters, "but it's obvious they don't have a case if the only thing they can do is destroy my credibility."

But Priscilla's story was ignored, as jurors, spectators and even prosecutors found her testimony implausible. District Attorney Tim Curry said, "If I never see Priscilla Davis again, it will be too soon."

Haynes' cross-examination of Beverly Bass followed a similar path, with similar success. After the state rested, the defense called a parade of witnesses to discredit prosecution witnesses and offer alternative theories for the killings other than Cullen's guilt.

Meanwhile, Judge Dowlen allowed Cullen to install a phone line in his office, and the judge's assistant gleefully oversaw Cullen's fan mail. A spare jury room was made available for the defense team's daily luncheon. As waiters in gold jackets served up inch-thick T-bone steaks, Cullen met with reporters as well as attorneys, investigators and business associates.

When it came time for final arguments to the jury, Haynes concluded, "The state's case is predicated on the testimony of Priscilla Lee Davis, who is not worthy." He took his seat amid scattered applause.

After four months of trial, the jury retired to deliberate. Less than four hours later, a verdict was returned. "We the jury, find the defendant...not guilty." Cullen Davis was free.

Amarillo's infatuation with all things Cullen was not over. A local TV news crew crashed Cullen's victory party at Rhett Butler's restaurant at Sixteenth and Butler, capturing the drunken celebrants on film. Haynes grabbed the microphone and continued his attack against Priscilla, "She is the most shameless, brazen hussy in all of humanity. She is a charlatan, a harlot, and a liar. She is a snake, unworthy of belief under oath. She is a dope fiend, a habitue of dope."

Everyone was there: the attorneys, the investigators, the secretaries, Cullen's business executives, reporters, even four of the jurors, all one big drunken throng. Cullen strutted among them.

One female juror explained her decision to acquit. "Rich men don't kill their wives. They hire someone else to do it."

Soon, even the courtroom bailiff joined the party. Then, the crowd was heard chanting "Dow-len! Dow-len! Dow-len!," as the judge entered the room. "Have a drink on us!," they insisted. Judge Dowlen consented and later took the place of honor next to Cullen at dinner.

The biggest murder trial in Amarillo's history was over, but the bizarre saga of Cullen Davis was not. In 1978, Cullen was accused of ordering the deaths of Priscilla and James Eidson, the judge in their Fort Worth divorce case. An employee acting in an undercover capacity for the FBI tape-recorded his conversation with Cullen in a Fort Worth parking lot.

"Do the judge and then his wife," Cullen said. Federal agents faked the judge's death, taking photos of him stuffed in the trunk of a car, "bloodied" with ketchup. The employee showed Cullen the photos. "I got Judge Eidson dead for you." Cullen replied, "Good." The informant said, "You want Beverly Bass killed next—quick, right?" Cullen answered, "All right."

Cullen claimed he merely played along with the plot in an attempt to eventually convince the employee to admit that Priscilla was to blame for the entire scheme. With Racehorse Haynes' help, Cullen was acquitted once again.

Most of the main players in the Cullen Davis saga are gone. Priscilla died of breast cancer at age fifty-nine, Haynes died at age ninety in 2017 and Judge Dowlen died in 2014 at age seventy-nine. Cullen, age eighty-nine in September 2022, lost most of his oil fortune in the 1980s and declared bankruptcy. He later became a born-again Christian and continues to live in Fort Worth.

15

LANDMARK LUBBOCK CASE PROTECTS DEFENDANT'S RIGHT TO COUNSEL

hree dozen outraged Lubbock lawyers passed the hat one evening in March 1989 and collected enough money to set in motion a lawsuit that would result in a landmark court decision on a defendant's right to counsel, *Stearnes v. Clinton*.*

The case began with a brutal murder in an east Lubbock home on September 10, 1987. The victims—Napoleon Ellison, Quinnie Smith and Vivian Webb—were felled by shotgun fire and blasts from an Uzi submachine gun. Police said the murders were drug related, and capital murder indictments were handed down against four young Black men: Damon Richardson, Michael Stearnes, Lambert Wilson and Rodney Childress.

Richardson—described as Lubbock's drug kingpin—hired prominent criminal defense lawyers Clifford and Mike Brown of Lubbock and Mike DeGeurin of Houston. The state's case was based primarily on the testimony of Anita Hansen—known as "Snowgirl"—who presented herself as Richardson's girlfriend. She testified that he ordered the hits and recruited Stearnes, Wilson and Childress to commit the murders. She claimed she witnessed the killings and said Richardson forced her to finish off one victim with an Uzi.

Richardson was convicted and sentenced to death. The remaining three defendants—all indigent and represented by appointed counsel—knew they were in big trouble. Stearnes, with Carlton McLarty and me as his lawyers, was next up for trial.

Three lawyers involved in the Stearnes case (*left to right*): David Botsford, Chuck Lanehart and Carlton McLarty. *Author's collection.*

Snowgirl had been held in "protective custody" until the verdict in the Richardson trial. After her release, Snowgirl called Carlton asking for legal advice. Carlton declined, but Snowgirl agreed to an interview. On February 28, 1989, he appeared at her home with another lawyer and a legal assistant armed with a tape recorder.

At first, Snowgirl cooperated and answered all of Carlton's questions. However, midway through the interview, she secretly called an assistant district attorney. The prosecutor soon appeared at Snowgirl's home with police and ended the interview. Carlton and I immediately filed a motion to take Snowgirl's deposition. However, at the March 2 hearing on the motion, something unexpected happened. The Lubbock County criminal district attorney, Travis Ware, alleged that Carlton had tampered with his "protected witness" and said the attorney had violated the CDA's rule "to ask permission before interviewing a state's witness."

Judge Thomas Clinton agreed, stating on the record that Carlton and I lacked experience to handle the case, and he fired us as Stearnes' attorneys. Stearnes defiantly stood to admonish Judge Clinton. "I ain't gonna stand for no shit like that!" The judge replied, "You keep a civil tongue in your mouth, or I will have you up for something else besides capital murder." Stearnes replied, "Well, this is wrong!"

Members of the Lubbock Criminal Defense Lawyers Association (LCDLA) agreed with Stearnes that Judge Clinton's ruling was very wrong. They held an emergency meeting that evening and decided to seek advice to challenge Clinton's intolerable decision: he had fired Stearnes' attorneys for effectively representing their client. About thirty-five lawyers donated money to send LCDLA representatives to Austin to meet with leaders of the Texas Criminal Defense Lawyers Association (TCDLA). In Austin, a plan was hatched to file a "writ of mandamus" in the Texas Court of Criminal Appeals to force the reinstatement of Stearnes' attorneys.

Austin lawyer David Botsford and Lubbock lawyer Ralph H. Brock volunteered pro bono on behalf of Stearnes and litigated the writ. LCDLA, TCDLA, the National Association of Criminal Defense Lawyers and the NAACP Legal Defense Fund all joined in the effort.

When the dust settled, the Texas Court of Criminal Appeals unanimously voted to grant mandamus relief in a momentous decision, *Stearnes v. Clinton*, holding that zealous representation requires even a court-appointed lawyer to interview witnesses, and "the power of the trial court to appoint counsel to represent indigent defendants does not carry with it the concomitant power to remove counsel at his discretionary whim." The court ordered the reinstatement of Carlton and me as Stearnes' attorneys.

Once back on the job, we filed a motion to disqualify Judge Clinton, which was granted. The new judge ordered Snowgirl to sit for a deposition, and she answered all of our questions. (In Texas criminal cases, the judge must grant permission for a deposition, and depositions are very rarely granted.)

At trial, Carlton and I demolished Snowgirl's credibility, and Stearnes was acquitted, exactly one year after we were fired. In the gallery, a crowd of lawyers applauded.

Revelations in the Stearnes trial helped clear the remaining two co-defendants. Richardson's death sentence was eventually set aside when the court ruled the prosecution withheld exculpatory evidence regarding Snowgirl's lack of credibility.

The 1989 case of *Stearnes v. Clinton* was hailed as a landmark decision and has since been cited as precedent in more than one hundred cases where judges have attempted to fire criminal defense lawyers over the objection of their clients.

*Caprock Chronicles editor Jack Becker authored this article with my help. I include this article with Jack's permission, and I have changed the perspective slightly.

PART III

MUSIC LEGENDS OF THE TEXAS PLAINS

From "Pretty Woman" to "Big Bad John"

16

DOWN BETWEEN THE RIVERS

Bob Wills' Early Days

Growing up in rural Texas, he was called Jim Rob, Jim Bob and, finally, just Bob, but James Robert Wills will always be celebrated as the "King of Western Swing."

John and Edna Wills' family, which would grow to ten children, moved to Hall County in 1913 and later bought a six-hundred-acre cotton farm known as "Down between the Rivers," bounded by the Prairie Dog Fork of the Red River and the Little Red River. Though rarely successful at farming, the Wills family became familiar throughout the Texas Plains as acclaimed musicians.

Born in 1905, eldest child Bob came by his fiddling talent naturally. His grandfather played violin, and his father was a champion fiddler. He first played in public at age ten at a "ranch dance," a common country event in which neighbors from miles around gathered at the host's ranch house for barbecue and traditional fiddle dance tunes. Popular songs were "Sally Goodin," "Eighth of January" and "Put Your Little Foot," among others. Bob, his father and brother Billy Jack wrote the blues-type tune "Faded Love," a favorite among the revelers.

Bob quickly absorbed country music styles, but he was also influenced by African American blues. As a child, Black kids were his earliest playmates, and they later picked cotton side by side. Bob was especially taken with their brass instruments and said he combined blues horns with traditional fiddle "because I've loved horns since I was a little boy."

He left school after the seventh grade. Between 1921 and 1926, Bob drifted about as a farmer, preacher, shine boy, carpenter, salesman and construction worker, but music was always a constant in his life.

The Wills family band continued to play for ranch dances, including gigs at the 6666 Ranch near Guthrie and the Matador Ranch in Motley County. Bob played his fiddle so long and hard he bruised his chin, and the wound festered. Doctors scraped the infection to the bone, leaving him with a scar he bore the rest of his life.

Bob developed a reputation for excesses of all varieties: drinking, gambling, fighting and general irresponsibility, and his performances became unpredictable. He failed to appear for engagements and sometimes showed up intoxicated. Fans marveled at how well he did in spite of his drunkenness and inconsistency.

He settled down after meeting a charming East Texas girl, Edna Posey, and they married in 1926. Bob decided picking cotton threatened his sensitive hands, which he knew were his future. He tried selling insurance and then completed barber school. In 1927, he became a barber in Roy, New Mexico, where he formed a band with talented Mexican American musicians. In Roy, Bob added to his style a third influence after traditional fiddle music and African American blues: Mexican mariachi sounds.

When Edna became pregnant in 1928, the couple returned to Hall County, settling in Turkey, population nine hundred. Bob barbered and grew to love the little city, later calling it "my hometown."

By age twenty-three, Bob had gained extraordinary popularity as an entertainer. Decades later, a fan compared his West Texas following to that of the Beatles. Teenage girls' common reaction to his trademark "Ah haa!" holler was described as "pandemonium." Older folks appreciated his music to the extent that residents near death would request they hear "Jim Bob Wills play one more time."

As his barber career gave way to music success, Bob succumbed to his old demons. One night in 1929, after attending an out-of-town ball game with friends, he returned to Turkey quite drunk. He was arrested and spent the night in jail. Though his fans were willing to forgive him, Bob was humiliated. He packed his bags, dropped by the family farm for goodbyes and headed east alone, never to live down between the rivers again.

Arriving in Fort Worth, Bob played fiddle, sang, cracked jokes and danced in minstrel shows. He sent for his wife and baby daughter and formed a band—the Light Crust Doughboys—performing regularly on live radio. With vocalist Milton Brown, he created a new sound, Western Swing, a big-

Bob Wills (*in all black*) and His Texas Playboys, 1947. *Courtesy of the Portal to Texas History.*

band fusion of fast-paced dance music combining country, polka, swing, Dixieland jazz, blues and mariachi styles.

After Brown left the Doughboys, Bob formed the Texas Playboys. They first recorded in Dallas in 1938, and their 1940 signature song "New San Antonio Rose" (with a hint of mariachi) sold a million records. Through the 1950s, Bob Wills and His Texas Playboys recorded hit after hit and relentlessly toured the nation, drawing huge crowds. Ultimately, Bob's popularity began to fade with the rise of rock 'n' roll.

Bob was married six times, divorced five times and fathered six children. He died at age seventy in 1975.

He was inducted into the Country Music Hall of Fame, Nashville Songwriters Hall of Fame and Rock & Roll Hall of Fame. His hometown of Turkey has hosted an annual Bob Wills Day since 1972.

17

ROY ORBISON'S EARLY YEARS

Overcoming West Texas Challenges

His iconic contemporary Buddy Holly often praised his South Plains heritage, but superstar rock balladeer Roy Orbison was critical of his own West Texas roots. Orbison said, "If you grow up in West Texas, there are a lot of ways to be lonely." There is little doubt that West Texas culture—and Roy's determination to overcome its challenges—played an inspirational role in his development as a singer-songwriter.

Roy's working-class parents chased jobs in the Texas oil industry, landing in the shantytown of Wink in 1946, when Roy was in grade school. The boy was small and homely, with protruding ears, cotton-colored hair and close-set pale blue eyes, which required thick eyeglasses from age four. His skin was sallow, and some wondered if he was albino. Classmates shunned and bullied Roy, and he was saddled with a derogatory nickname, "Facetus."

"It's really hard to describe," Roy later said about growing up in Wink. "It was macho guys working in the oil field, and football, and oil and grease and sand, and being a stud and being cool. I got out of there as quick as I could, and I resented having to be there. But it was a great education. It was tough as could be."

By the time Roy reached junior high school, everyone recognized his musical talent. He had played the guitar since age six and sang at every opportunity, winning several talent contests starting at age ten. Roy was not popular in school, but he was welcome in the prestigious Wink marching band, where he played the baritone horn. He formed his own band, the Wink Westerners, playing gigs—mostly country and popular tunes—throughout the region.

Roy Orbison (*second from left*), pictured with the Teen Kings, circa 1956. *Public domain.*

After graduation in 1954, Roy studied geology at North Texas State College, but then he heard Elvis Presley and traded college for rock 'n' roll. The Westerners became the Teen Kings, exploring the rockabilly craze. Soon—with help from Clovis, New Mexico record producer Norman Petty—he recorded a minor hit, "Oobie Doobie." Roy headed to Nashville and Sun Records, Elvis' record company.

Meanwhile, Roy developed relationships with future legendary West Texas musicians. Roy played Lawson's Roller Rink in Lubbock on weekends when Buddy Holly was not booked. Waylon Jennings remembered, "Me, Buddy Holly, Roy Orbison…and Sonny Curtis, were at the bus station in Lubbock. We had a quarter and Sonny put it in the jukebox and played Chet Atkins, and that's about all we had was a quarter. We snuck into a Sonny James/Jim Reeves show."

Early in his career, Roy dyed his light hair jet black. He was inspired by Buddy Holly's bold eyeglasses and later adopted his own distinctive look, dark Ray-Ban sunglasses.

Claudette Frady was a stunning teenage beauty whose parents lived in Odessa and later in Lubbock. Soon after they met, Roy and Claudette married, settling in Wink in 1957. In her honor, Roy wrote a song he offered to the Everly Brothers. Their 1958 rendition of "Claudette" was a hit. With song royalties, Roy bought the most expensive new Cadillac in Odessa, with sweeping green tailfins. In Wink, everyone noticed.

When Roy's recording career with Sun stalled, he signed with Monument Records in 1959. His career took off in 1961 with "Only the Lonely," which reached number two on the U.S. charts and number one in Britain. It sold more than three million copies, making Roy an international recording star. The song was followed by a string of hits in the 1960s, including "Crying," "Running Scared" and "Oh, Pretty Woman."

Soon, Roy moved Claudette and his growing family to Nashville and then hit the road, touring internationally. He shared billings with the Beatles as the hits kept coming.

Tragedy struck in 1966. Claudette was killed in a motorcycle accident, and two years later, two of their three sons died in a house fire. Roy's career declined during the 1970s, but he enjoyed a resurgence in the 1980s.

In 1987, Roy came home for the Midland-Odessa Oil Aid Concert, where he was greeted by an entourage from Wink. He signed autographs and posed for photos, saying, "It's good to be back in West Texas. You need to be reminded of your roots." But to the people of Wink, he was still Facetus.

Roy said, "That's the way people are out there. I'm sure they think of me as just a good ole boy, but I always thought the best thing to come out of Wink was me and the 1952 state championship football team."

Just as his star shone the brightest—his 1988 musical collaboration with George Harrison, Bob Dylan, Tom Petty and Jeff Lynne as part of the Traveling Wilburys—Roy suffered a heart attack and died in December of that year. He was fifty-two years old.

Unlike Buddy Holly, who was buried in his beloved hometown of Lubbock, Orbison was laid to rest in California.

18

THE GOOD-HEARTED WOMEN OF WEST TEXAS

Peggy Sue, Claudette and Others

One way to a woman's heart is verse, especially verse about the target of affection. Music icons of West Texas—familiar with the concept—produced great love songs glorifying their girlfriends.

Buddy Holly met Peggy Sue Gerron in 1956 when she was a sophomore at Lubbock High School. As she walked to the band room, Buddy was rushing to the auditorium to perform at an assembly. They crashed together in the hallway, and she fell to the floor, her books scattering and her poodle skirt rising over her knees. One arm carried his guitar, the other his amp. "I'm terribly sorry, but I don't have time to pick you up," Buddy said.

In early 1957, Buddy teamed with drummer Jerry "J.I." Allison and Joe B. Mauldin to form the Crickets, and they released the number-one hit song "That'll Be the Day" in May 1957.

Meanwhile, J.I. and Peggy Sue began dating, but they broke up. In the summer of 1957, the band rehearsed its new song, "Cindy Lou." Cindy Lou was Buddy's niece, but the title was changed to "Peggy Sue" at J.I.'s request. The song, released in July, jumped to number three on the pop charts.

When blond, blue-eyed Peggy Sue heard the song, she said she was "so embarrassed I could have died." Nevertheless, J.I. and Peggy Sue reconciled and married in 1958, inspiring a sequel, "Peggy Sue Got Married," recorded in 1959.

The song "Peggy Sue," featuring J.I. playing paradiddles on drums throughout, was inducted into the Grammy Hall of Fame in 1999.

Peggy Sue and J.I. divorced in 1964. She moved to California and remarried. She and her husband opened a plumbing company and raised two children. Peggy Sue returned to Lubbock in 1995, where she lived until her death in 2018 at age seventy-eight. J.I. Allison, age eighty-two in 2022—the last survivor of the original Crickets—lives in Nashville.

Roy Orbison was raised in Wink, a tiny West Texas oil town. In nearby Odessa, teenager Claudette Frady lived with her family. Considered the prettiest girl in West Texas, Claudette was tall, with dark hair, bright hazel eyes and a shapely build. Some compared her beauty to that of Elizabeth Taylor.

Roy met Claudette as he was gaining fame for his minor hit "Oobie Doobie." They married in 1957, when Claudette was sixteen and Roy was twenty-one. Soon, he wrote a song, "Claudette," which he offered to the hottest country-rock duo in the country, the Everly Brothers, who released "Claudette" in 1958 on the B side of their number-one single, "All I Have to Do Is Dream." "Claudette" reached number thirty. It jumpstarted Roy's brilliant career as a singer-songwriter, and the couple moved from Wink to Nashville.

In July 1964, Roy was at home working with songwriting collaborator Bill Dees when Claudette appeared. She was headed to town. "Give me some money, honey," she said. Roy responded, "What do you need it for?" Bill said, "A pretty woman never needs any money." Minutes later, the inspired songwriters completed what would become Roy's masterpiece, "Oh, Pretty Woman." The song was a number-one megahit. In 2008, the Library of Congress selected the song for preservation in the National Recording Registry.

Tragically, Claudette was killed in a motorcycle accident in 1966 at age twenty-four. Two years later, two of Roy and Claudette's three young sons died when fire destroyed their Nashville home. Heartbroken, Orbison's career foundered in the 1970s, but he rebounded in the 1980s. He suffered a fatal heart attack in 1988 at age fifty-two.

Country star Waylon Jennings, a native of Littlefield, was inspired by a TV spot about singer Tina Turner, a "good hearted woman loving two-timing men," a reference to her abusive husband, Ike Turner. During a poker game, Waylon discussed his idea with his buddy, singer-songwriter Willie Nelson. Undistracted from their gambling, the two traded thoughts over cards and put a song together as Willie's wife, Connie, wrote down the lyrics.

"Good Hearted Woman," recorded by Waylon and Willie in 1971 and remixed in 1975, hit number one on the country charts, launching the

Claudette and Roy Orbison, circa 1960. *Public domain.*

Outlaw Country movement. The song won the Country Music Association's Single of the Year award in 1976. Waylon died in 2002 at age sixty-four; octogenarians Willie and Tina still perform.

In 1962, Ray Hildebrand was a budding musician and a scholarship basketball player for Howard Payne University in Brownwood. A teammate asked Ray to write a song for his girlfriend, Paula. Inspired by an Annette

Funicello song, "Tall Paul," Ray wrote "Hey Paula," Jill Jackson was the niece of the owner of the boardinghouse where Ray lived. Calling themselves "Paul and Paula," Ray and Jill recorded the song, and it reached number one on the charts in 1963. Ray and Jill still occasionally perform together, but no one seems to know what happened to Paula.

19

PLAINVIEW'S JIMMY DEAN

One Helluva Man

H igh school dropout Jimmy Dean overcame poverty and an abusive father to become one of a few who have excelled and gained fame in multiple professions: music, acting and big business.

Born in Olton, Texas, in 1928, he was raised in Seth Ward, a neighborhood on the outskirts of Plainview. He came from a long line of West Texas farmers, but Jimmy said his father, G.L. Dean, tried "anything to get out of doing an honest day's work" as a songwriter, inventor, singer, preacher and author. "He beat the hell out of me a lot," Jimmy said, and deserted the family when the boy was age eleven.

"We were one of the poorest families around," Jimmy said. His mother, Ruth, did the best she could raising Jimmy and younger brother Don, but Jimmy was obliged to travel by foot or on horseback, and "nobody wore shirts made out of sugar sacks but me. I was an outcast and the butt of other kids' jokes." He worked in cotton fields "pulling bolls" from age six.

Jimmy attended Seth Ward Baptist Church, where he became interested in music, and his mother taught him piano chords. He bought a thirty-five-dollar accordion and learned to play. "I fell in love with that accordion because it had this silver diamond in the bellows with lots of mother of pearl, and I thought it was one of the prettiest things I'd ever seen."

At age sixteen, Jimmy dropped out of Plainview High School and soon enlisted in the U.S. Air Force. While stationed in Washington, D.C., he joined the house band at Harry's Tavern. "I was hooked," he said. He pursued music gigs throughout his military career, sending extra money home.

After the service, Jimmy hosted a radio show at a Washington, D.C. station, where he and his band performed. He moved to national television and in 1958–59 hosted *The Jimmy Dean Show*, a Monday–Saturday afternoon variety program on CBS.

In 1961, Jimmy's hit single "Big Bad John" shot to number one on every music chart, sold a million records and earned him a Grammy. He recorded many more Top 40 songs, and in 1976, "I.O.U."—a tribute to his mother—sold a million copies.

Meanwhile, Jimmy often appeared on TV programs. He revived *The Jimmy Dean Show* in the mid-1960s and, in 1966, turned to acting. He appeared

Jimmy Dean, circa 1958. *Public domain.*

in various roles on *Daniel Boone*, *Fantasy Island* and *J.J. Starbuck* and played reclusive Las Vegas billionaire Willard Whyte in the James Bond movie *Diamonds Are Forever*.

"I've had a lot of friends in the entertainment industry and have known many of them who have made a fortune and ended up broke," Jimmy said. "You hear about them all the time, and I swore I'd never be one of them."

Over the years, he invested in banks, limousine companies, a lime grove, a Christmas tree farm, restaurants, real estate, music publishing and racehorses. When asked why he got into business, he joked, "If you had ever seen my act, you would have realized that diversification was imperative."

In 1965, he bought a hog farm in Edmonson, near Plainview, and named it "The Jimmy Dean Pig Parlor." The business failed, but in 1968, while eating breakfast with brother Don in a Plainview diner, "I reached in my mouth and pulled out a piece of gristle about the size of the tip of your little finger. I said to Don, 'You know, there's got to be room in this country for a good quality sausage.'"

Soon, the brothers established the Jimmy Dean Meat Company, a thirty-four-thousand-square-foot packing plant in Plainview, the only venture of its kind in the world: a self-contained plant that could process four hundred hogs a day.

The company became the number-one seller of breakfast sausage in America, with Jimmy as its folksy spokesman on television commercials airing seemingly everywhere. About 150 employees earned an annual payroll of more than $3 million.

Unfortunately, the business eventually outgrew Plainview, and the operation moved to Iowa in 1978. "It hurt" to move his business out of Plainview, Jimmy said. In 1984, Consolidated Foods purchased Jimmy's company for $80 million (worth $230 million in 2022), and he continued as spokesman. Occasionally, his image still drifts across the TV screen in sausage commercials.

Jimmy said, "The harder I worked the luckier I got." He was influenced by his mother's advice: "It's nice to be important, but it's more important to be nice."

The high school dropout who had been ridiculed for his poverty as a youngster remained closely connected to his hometown of Plainview. In 2008, he donated $1 million to the city's Wayland Baptist University.

Jimmy died at age eighty-one in 2010. He was posthumously inducted into the Country Music Hall of Fame a few months later. His epitaph reads "Here Lies One Hell of a Man," a line paraphrased from his megahit "Big Bad John."

20

"LITTLEFIELD GETS IN YOUR SOUL"

Waylon Jennings' Early Years on the South Plains

They say you can stand in Littlefield and count the folks in Levelland, twenty miles away. The pancake-flat South Plains agricultural town of Littlefield was home to about 3,500 people when Wayland Jennings was born there in 1937.

His birth certificate read "Wayland." Then his mother learned the name was connected to Wayland Baptist University in nearby Plainview, and Lorene Jennings—a devout member of the Church of Christ—promptly changed his name to Waylon.

In his autobiography, Waylon described his family of subsistence farmers as "dirt poor, with the floor to prove it." Waylon's family shared a two-room, rat-infested shack with uncles, aunts and cousins, twelve people in all.

From the time he was a little boy, Waylon spent summers barefoot, pulling cotton in scorching heat, with gnats swarming at his eyes, the insects seeking moisture. He hated it and would eventually walk away as a teenager.

He was raised in the conservative Church of Christ. "I thought, man, I'm going to hell, 'cause everything they tell me is a big sin is something I like a lot. A lot."

His parents were musical. William, his father, played harmonica and guitar. His mother taught him guitar chords, and they often sang together. "She put all her soul into her singing; she could be so moved by it."

Waylon remembered everyone loving life in Littlefield. "It's a rough place to be, if you want to know the truth, but if you survive Littlefield, then you can pretty well handle the rest of the world. I have to go back every once in

Waylon Jennings, 1956. *Courtesy of James Jennings.*

a while, just to see where I've been and who I am. I don't know why that is.

"Littlefield gets in your soul, in your blood, the same way sand gets in your craw. I think that's part of my sound. All the damn sand I swallowed is in my singing."

Waylon did not do well in school. He was expelled from music class for "lack of talent" and almost got in a fight with his principal in tenth grade. One day, the school bully threatened him. Waylon "kicked his butt bad. I liked it so well I went and found him twice more that day and whipped him again." He dropped out at age sixteen.

A series of menial jobs followed: he stocked dry goods, unloaded grocery trucks, jackhammered cars at a body shop, pumped gas at a service station and was a projectionist at a Spanish-language movie theater.

Waylon began taking his guitar out in public. He performed for free at the Palace Theater and for the Jaycees and Lions Club. He won a talent show in Muleshoe, then made the rounds, singing "Hey Joe" on Lubbock's KLBK-TV.

At age fourteen, Waylon began performing on KVOW radio in Littlefield, and the station hired him as a disc jockey, spinning country, classics, waltzes and all other styles of music. "The whole station was held together with barbed wire and spit, and I'd been working there since I was barely a teenager. By the time 1956 was underway, I was almost an old pro. I knew I would be leaving Littlefield soon."

The racist station manager fired him for playing Little Richard rock 'n' roll tunes, and Waylon headed for Lubbock, where he found work as a DJ at KDAV and KLLL. Waylon often performed at country radio station KDAV, where he met Buddy Holly. Waylon began attending Buddy's performances on KDAV's *Sunday Party*.

Waylon said Buddy was "the first guy who had confidence in me." Buddy said, "There's no doubt you're going to be a star. I know. The way you sing, there's no limit. You can sing pop, you can sing rock, and you can sing country."

99

Buddy mentored Waylon and hired him as bassist for his band for the tragic Winter Dance Party tour of 1959. Waylon famously gave up his seat to The Big Bopper on Buddy's charter flight, which crashed on February 3 near Clear Lake, Iowa.

Waylon was always haunted by a conversation with Buddy that night. "You're not going with me tonight, huh?" Buddy asked. "Did you chicken out?"

Waylon replied: "No, I'm not scared. The Big Bopper just wanted to go."

"Well," Buddy said, grinning, "I hope your damned bus freezes up again."

Waylon replied, "Well, I hope your ol' plane crashes."

Waylon went on to form a rockabilly band, The Waylors, and eventually inked an RCA recording contract. After gaining creative control of his music, he delivered a long string of acclaimed country singles and albums. With his friend Willie Nelson, Waylon is credited with establishing the Outlaw Country movement in the 1970s.

In 2001, he was inducted into the Country Music Hall of Fame. Waylon lived a hard-partying life. He eventually recovered from drug addiction and kicked a six-pack-a-day smoking habit. He died in 2002 at age sixty-four from complications of diabetes.

Waylon Jennings remains Littlefield's favorite son.

21

JOHN "DUTCH" DENVER AT TEXAS TECH

I n his 1994 autobiography, John Denver wrote but a handful of paragraphs about his education at Texas Tech, but he remembered Tech as a "great environment for an artist." College friends fondly remember the budding, bespectacled troubadour who spent just a couple of years in Lubbock in the early 1960s.

Henry John Deutschendorf Jr. was born in Roswell, New Mexico, in 1943. An "air force brat," he and his family relocated to various military destinations during his early years. His grandmother gave him his first guitar, and by the time he was a teenager, he had mastered the instrument.

After graduation from Arlington Heights High School, John remembered, "College was a shaky proposition....All I knew about college was that you went there after high school."

In the fall of 1961, John's father drove him to Lubbock and advised the youngster: "You know, you've got a talent. You can play guitar and you can sing. Not everybody can do that. But that does not make you any better than anybody else...remember that."

He enrolled in Texas Technological College as an architecture major. After John moved into his dormitory, Gaston Hall, most folks knew him by the nickname "Dutch."

One of Dutch's friends was Kent Hance, who forty-one years later served as chancellor of the Texas Tech University system. Dutch pledged Delta Tau Delta, and Kent was the fraternity president.

The fraternity had grade requirements, and Dutch's marks were always below par. Kent said: "He was more interested in music and impressing young ladies on campus. I told that boy to throw that guitar away." But the Delts eventually made him an honorary member, and Dutch performed at fraternity functions, eventually earning a following on campus and around Lubbock.

"What made me happy—and what kept me at school—was the music I was making, and sometimes getting paid for," John said. "I sang with a group called the Alpine Trio, and sometimes I sang by myself. Even in the dorm, I was the troubadour. You could always find me in my room at the head of the stairs. My dorm-mates liked to share their stories of conquest and plunder, and I liked to listen while playing the guitar."

Fellow student George Chaffee and Dutch joined the Alpine Trio about the same time, and George said that John's skills were impressive. "The first time I met him…I knew this really fancy and fairly difficult finger-picking introduction that Peter, Paul and Mary had used on a song," George remembered. "So I started playing that as we were getting tuned up. And John just started playing it right along with me, just grinning like crazy.

"Musically he had the skills, and then confidence-wise, you know, he wasn't really cocky," George said. "He just knew that he was an excellent singer, performer. He knew that he could entertain well."

Dow Patterson, a fellow architecture major, performed with Dutch. He remembered Dutch sitting on a yellow Coca-Cola crate in a dormitory shower, grinning, singing and playing guitar. He told Dow he liked the acoustics in the community restroom. "I never would have guessed that smiling kid would become a folk music legend," Dow said.

John Denver (*in glasses*), February 8, 1964, at Kappa Alpha Grubbers Ball. Note the date one day before the Beatles first performed on *The Ed Sullivan Show. Courtesy of Dow Patterson.*

Dutch became inconsolable after the Kennedy assassination in November 1963. Soon after he returned to Tech after the semester break, he decided to head to California. "Everybody I knew, from my professors to my friends, told me I was making the biggest mistake of my life."

George Chaffee remembered, "We were at the student union building the last time I saw him. He had a white…1956 Chevrolet, and it was packed to the gills with his instruments…everything he had. I remember walking him out to the car…saying goodbye and we all shook his hand, slapped him on the back and watched him drive away. And I thought, 'That poor guy.'"

Soon after arriving in Los Angeles, the twenty-year-old Texas Tech dropout morphed into John Denver, singer-songwriter. He joined the Chad Mitchell Trio in 1965.

By 1969, John was a solo performer, released an album on RCA, and one of his songs was covered by folk superstars Peter, Paul and Mary. "Leaving on a Jet Plane" became a number-one hit. John recorded his first hit, "Take Me Home, Country Roads," in 1971, followed by a string of other hits. He became one of the most popular performers of the 1970s.

His career flourished: acting (*Oh, God!*), successful TV variety shows, guest-host of *The Tonight Show*, Country Music Association Entertainer of the Year. In 1996, he was inducted into the Songwriters Hall of Fame. John Denver—"Dutch" to his Tech friends—died when his experimental plane crashed in 1997. He was fifty-three.

PART IV

GRIDIRON GREATS AND HARDWOOD HEROES OF THE TEXAS PLAINS

22

THE BULL THAT BECAME BBQ

The True Story of Texas Tech's First Mascot

The story of Texas Tech's first mascot is familiar. Arch Lamb, a member of Tech's spirit organization the Saddle Tramps, dreamed up the idea in 1936. That fall, George Tate—wearing a scarlet satin cape—led the Matadors onto the football field riding a horse borrowed from the Tech barn, and the Matadors became known as the Red Raiders. The tradition lapsed until the first masked rider, Joe Kirk Fulton, charged across the field riding the magnificent steed Blackie at the 1954 Gator Bowl.

But the familiar version of the first Tech mascot is inaccurate. The first mascot was not a masked rider on a horse. Tech's first mascot was instead a bull with a braggadocios brand. He became barbecue.

The story begins with Marvin Warlick. Born in Florida in 1892, he was the son of an itinerant Methodist minister. After attending Byrnes Business College in Tyler, Warlick bumped about the country before arriving in Lubbock in about 1915 to work in the Lubbock County clerk's office. He married Thelma Caraway, and they began raising a family. In 1917, Warlick was drafted into the army to serve in Europe during World War I, leaving Thelma in Lubbock.

Upon his return, Warlick took up farming west of town, raising grain, cotton, swine and cattle. One of the couple's children, Tom, was born in a farmhouse on land that would one day accommodate a great university.

Warlick was elected Lubbock County commissioner and supervised the building of a road to the site offered for a new school, Texas Technological College. When Lubbock landed the much-coveted institution in 1923, an editorial claimed that Warlick's road (now western Broadway Avenue) deserved much of the credit.

Tech's first president, Dr. Paul Horn, recruited Warlick as farm superintendent in the School of Agriculture. He helped clear the two thousand acres, making way for a proper college campus. He participated in the ceremony of driving the first stake to locate the Texas Tech Administration Building.

When Tech opened in the fall of 1925, Warlick became buildings and grounds superintendent. He leveled a spot on campus for a practice football field. As a reward, Coach Ewing Freeland gave him the privilege of inflating the first football used by the team, nicknamed the Matadors.

Warlick's memoirs recount the appearance of Tech's first mascot:

> For a mascot I gave the team a nice thoroughbred Hereford bull yearling. The team lost the first game but won the second one by the score of 30 to zero. It was decided that this score should be branded on the side of our mascot at the next game. This was done during halftime at the game that was played on the [Panhandle South Plains] fairgrounds. Then it was decided that it would be fun for some of the students to try to ride the mad bull. I offered a ten-dollar bill to any successful rider. Several tried but were promptly dumped. This rodeo was more popular with the large crowd than the football game. It was repeated thereafter at every game. We took our mascot in the baggage car on all trips.

The 30–0 game described by Warlick as Tech's second was in fact its third, against Montezuma College. The first two games were ties—not losses—against McMurry and Austin College. The 1925 football record was 6-1-2, including a 120–0 home win against Wayland Baptist, Tech's only 100-point win.

In a 0–30 loss at Howard Payne late in the season, Warlick noticed

> a cowboy was collecting a group together and pointing to our mascot…they planned on seizing our bull. I hurriedly collected a group of Tech boys and we rushed the bull out a back gate and headed for the depot some ten blocks away. We were no sooner in the street than here came the thieves followed by both student bodies. The fact that the baggage door was open saved our mascot, for the baggage master quickly closed and locked the door. Fistfights with bloody noses followed.

The first Texas Tech football team poses with their mascot. *Courtesy of Dr. Brian Carr.*

After the season ended, the animal was butchered and barbecued for a team banquet. The bull's branded hide was to be displayed in the trophy room, but the hide was lost.

There is no evidence of an official Tech mascot for another twenty-five years. Briefly in the early 1950s, a sleek Angus bull mascot, the "Black Invader," appeared at football games, but it proved to be a jinx, with Tech losing most games. After Fulton rode Blackie at the Gator Bowl in 1954, the Masked Rider became the official Texas Tech mascot.

Warlick died in 1984. Descendants of his extended family include many distinguished Lubbock citizens: former Texas attorney general Waggoner Carr, lawyer Warlick Carr, pediatrician Dr. Robert Carr, former Tech cheerleader Virginia Carr Carter, orthopedist Dr. Robert V. Carr, psychologist Dr. Brian Carr, dentist Dr. David Carr and RN Julie Carr Coffern—all Tech graduates.

23

ELMER THE GREAT

Texas Tech's First Sports Superstar

Elmer Tarbox—football champion, war hero, businessman and statesman—arose from humble beginnings in the Texas Panhandle hamlet of Higgins, a town too tiny to field a football team. Born in 1916, Elmer arrived at Texas Technological College in 1935 having witnessed just one gridiron game. He left as Tech's first sports superstar.

Elmer worked part-time at a downtown service station, washed dishes at the campus cafeteria and signed up for athletics at Tech because he heard players were fed for free. He was a football "walk-on," starting for Coach Pete Cawthon's Red Raiders, and between 1936 and 1938, he also lettered in basketball and track and boxing in the off-season. By the time he graduated, he was known as "Elmer the Great."

Elmer played offense and defense—halfback and cornerback—helping Tech to its first football conference championship (1937 in the Border Conference) and bowl game (a 7–6 loss in the 1938 Sun Bowl to West Virginia).

During the 1938 season, Elmer was the best player on Tech's undefeated football team, and his accomplishments that year were extraordinary, including eleven intercepted passes, an NCAA record for forty-four years. His other 1938 national records: seventh in rushing yards, tenth in pass receptions and first in yards per catch. He scored four touchdowns in a single game, a Tech record for forty years. He was an honorable mention All-America selection, and his team was ranked eleventh in final football polls.

In the 1939 Cotton Bowl, Tech faced an underdog, California's St. Mary's Gaels, but the Red Raiders suffered three turnovers and were upset, 20–13. Elmer caught a touchdown pass and was named co-MVP of the game.

During his Tech career, he was elected president of his junior and senior classes and taught Sunday school at Lubbock's First United Methodist Church, drawing packed classes of kids wanting to rub elbows with a football star.

Elmer earned his bachelor of business arts degree in 1939. He was the eighteenth pick in the 1939 NFL draft, chosen by the Cleveland Rams, but he never played professional football. Service to country became his priority.

In July 1940, before the beginning of World War II, Elmer volunteered for the U.S. Army Air Corps. Trained to pilot B-25 bombers, he was sent to the China-Burma-India sector, flying "The Hump" over the Himalayas as a member of General Claire Lee Chennault's "Flying Tigers."

Elmer Tarbox, 1939. *Courtesy of the Lubbock Avalanche-Journal.*

On one such mission, as Elmer was flying low through a mountain pass, Japanese anti-aircraft fire sent shrapnel through both of his legs. He was hospitalized and offered a chance to convalesce in the United States, but he decided to stay in India, where he oversaw armament and bomb site maintenance.

Elmer also helped modify the B-25 "wobble gun," featuring a rotating barrel at the stern that sprayed bullets at enemy aircraft approaching from the rear. The modifications vastly improved the firepower of gunners, saving American lives wherever the B-25 was in use.

By the end of the war, Elmer had been promoted to lieutenant colonel and was awarded the Silver Star for gallantry in action, the Air Medal for heroic and meritorious achievement while participating in aerial flight and the Purple Heart.

Elmer married the former Maxine Barnett, whom he had met at church in Higgins, and when he left the military, they returned to Lubbock. He worked for a local auto dealership and operated Lubbock's first drive-in movie theater, located in the northwest part of town.

Meanwhile, the couple began to develop an ankle-and-wrist weight device to strengthen athletes. As a player, Elmer observed that mud that stuck to football players' shoes added weight and caused fatigue to already tired muscles, but the benefits were visible weeks later in stronger ankles with better muscle tone.

In 1957, he began manufacturing "Elmer's Weights," which fastened to an athlete's ankles for weight training. It was a home industry at first, with the family fireplace used to melt lead ballasts as Elmer and Maxine sewed leather pouches and bindings in place. Elmer quit his job at the auto dealership to promote his product as far away as Europe. Initially, NFL Hall of Famer Bobby Layne served as the company's vice-president.

Sears, Roebuck & Company began placing large orders for Elmer's Weights, which were featured in the Sears catalogue. The family subsequently acquired property in Wolfforth and opened a factory.

In 1966, Elmer was elected to the Texas House of Representatives and served in the legislature for the next ten years. During his term, he helped establish the Texas Tech University School of Law and what is now the Texas Tech University Health Sciences Center (TTUHSC).

Elmer and Maxine raised four children. Elmer suffered from Parkinson's disease, and in 1972, he founded the Tarbox Parkinson's Disease Institute at TTUHSC. Maxine died in 1978, and Elmer died, of complications from Parkinson's, in 1987.

In August 2021, Elmer was inducted—much too late—into Tech's Football Ring of Honor. Athletic Director Kirby Hocutt said, "He was truly the Texas Tech version of Jim Thorpe."

24

LUBBOCK'S GREATEST GENERATION

The 1939 Lubbock High School Football Champions

The Lubbock High School (LHS) football team faced incredible obstacles on the way to the 1939 Texas schoolboy championship. The team's thirty-two boys, shaped by the Great Depression, would help win World War II as men and then go on to help shape the America we know today.

In the 1930s, Lubbock was an isolated South Plains town of about thirty thousand people, a small agricultural hub suffering from double-whammy disasters: the Dust Bowl and the Depression. A few Lubbock kids who overcame these challenges grew up oblivious to the challenges they would overcome as men.

Some met in grade school. Almost all played football together in junior high. By 1938, they were members of the Lubbock High School Westerners football team, and their story is one of the most compelling in sports history.

Under the direction of Coach Weldon Chapman, the Westerners reached the 1938 Texas schoolboy football championship, losing to Corpus Christi, 20–6. It was an era when all high schools competed against one another, regardless of size. Little LHS—with only 270 seniors—was often pitted against much larger high schools.

In the late summer of 1939, "Coach Chap" held practice two hundred miles east in Cisco to protect players from girlfriends and other diversions. It was described as a "football hell-hole."

"What I remember were the workouts…twice daily, in pads, and with no water or water breaks. Kids would die if they had to do that now," said running back Billy Wright many years later.

The boys loved their coach, despite his tough drills. Chapman suffered from various illnesses for years, and in the fall of 1939, a throat ailment worsened. Chapman's voice was barely audible, but his message never went unheard. "You could barely hear him, but when he started talking, it would get so quiet you could hear a pin drop," tackle Pat Farris remembered. "We wanted to hear what he had to say because we knew it would help us."

The start of the season was a disaster. With an average player weight of 156 pounds, the "Thin Gold and Black" team lost three games, won a game and tied a game.

Coach Chapman's condition worsened, and his team was riddled with injuries. The night before the first district game, at least six players spent all or part of the night in the hospital.

The next afternoon at Tech Stadium, the Westerners upset the mighty Pampa Harvesters, 6–0. After that, only two opponents would score against the Westerners, which met a more heavily favored squad in every game.

The next week, with Coach Chap in the hospital, LHS pummeled Borger, 40–0. As the coach's condition turned critical, assistants J.G. "Goober" Keyes and Walker Nichols directed the team.

On November 11, 1939, seconds after the end of the Westerners' 19–0 upset of the Plainview Bulldogs, a nurse walked into Coach Chapman's hospital room and told him the score. He smiled and then died, age thirty-seven.

The following Monday, the team was bused to Cisco for the funeral of the "Greatest Gentleman in Football" amid a host of friends and relatives. They solemnly returned to Lubbock to prepare for the rest of the season.

In spectacular fashion, LHS beat Hobbs, Amarillo, Electra, Sweetwater and Dallas Woodrow Wilson. Once again, the Westerners gained the right to play for the state championship. A sportswriter dubbed them the "Cinderella Kids," a nickname the team and the public embraced.

On a cold, blustery Saturday, December 30, at the Cotton Bowl, the Westerners faced the formidable Waco Tigers, winners of four previous state titles. The sturdy Tigers outweighed Lubbock's players by an average of thirteen pounds per man.

With hefty high-top cleats, flimsy leather helmets and no face masks, the Westerners' gritty starting eleven played virtually every down—offense,

Beloved coach Weldon Chapman died midway through the 1939 season. *1940 LHS yearbook.*

defense and special teams—with only one substitution. Lubbock led, 13–0, after the second quarter, and at halftime the LHS pep squad spelled out "Chap" on the field. But Waco scored 14 points in the third quarter to take the lead.

In the fourth quarter, the Westerners won the game on a twenty-eight-yard run by co-captain Howard Alford. Pete Cawthon furnished the block that paved the way. It was a 20–13 win that garnered acclaim throughout the state and beyond as one of the greatest victories in schoolboy football history.

After the game, the Cinderella Kids escorted Coach Chapman's widow, Minnie, onto the field and presented her with the state football championship trophy. The prize eventually went missing and did not appear in the LHS trophy case for decades.

It was an effort that grabbed the headlines and heartstrings of an entire state. Ministers and others cited the team's dedication as an example of what faith and hard work can achieve.

By the end of 1939, Nazi Germany had occupied Poland and Japan had taken China. Two years later, the Cinderella Kids were men confronted with a new challenge, World War II.

They hung up their cleats after winning the 1939 Texas state football championship, unaware they would soon be trading their flimsy leather helmets for steel armor. The Cinderella Kids, these thirty-two boys of the victorious Lubbock High School team, had no reason to believe their futures would be different from those of their fathers: perhaps graduation, farming, menial jobs, maybe college. The Dust Bowl and Depression-afflicted South Plains seemed to offer few opportunities.

But by the time Lubbock High graduation ceremonies were held in May 1940, Germany had invaded much of Europe and Japanese forces threatened the Pacific. The Japanese attack on Pearl Harbor forced the United States into war on December 7, 1941, and almost all of the LHS football champions—now full-grown men—enthusiastically entered the fray. War would dramatically change their lives and those of their contemporaries. They became known as the Greatest Generation.

On Sundays during World War II, the *Lubbock Avalanche-Journal* published full-page updates on South Plains servicemen and women, including many references to the Cinderella Kids.

The foundation of the Westerners' pass defense, L.A. Storrs, entered the service in May 1943, the *A-J* reported. Later, the army sent him to Baylor Medical School.

Sometimes, the articles brought bad news. Jack Lovin, a 141-pound back, had been a fighter and a hustler for the '39 team. "Lt. Jack Lovin…has been reported…a prisoner of war in Germany," according to the June 10, 1943 account. "He…was reported to have been in on the bombing of the dams in Ruhr valley."

On August 15, 1943, it was reported: "Sgt. R.E. Jones Jr. is stationed at the Army Air Forces Instrument Training School at Bryan. He was a member of the Westerner football squads of 1938 and the state champions of 1939. He enlisted in the Army in February 1942."

James Barker, whose pass-catching ability made him a constant threat for LHS, was the subject of a November 7, 1943 story. "Aviation student James Barker, 22…has been stationed at the University of Arkansas for four months."

Lieutenant Pat Farris, All-State tackle on the '39 LHS squad, received his wings as a bombardier from Midland Army Airfield on January 15, 1944.

The most dependable lineman of the 1939 Westerners was James Merriman, who was promoted to first lieutenant in the air branch of the Marines in March 1944. "He recently looked across the chow table to discover a former football teammate, Lt. Leete Jackson Jr. Merriman barely recognized Leete, who had a crossed *T* shaved into his hair." The symbol was not an homage to the Red Raiders, but a sign that he had crossed the 180th meridian.

The worst news came on March 30, 1944. "Mr. and Mrs. Henry G. Lawson…have been informed of the death of their son, Lt. Henry Neil Lawson, 21, in a plane crash.…Lawson was a Marine flyer." He was a 141-pound reserve tackle for the '39 Westerners, the only Cinderella Kid who died in the war.

Tackle Floyd Ward fought injuries during the LHS championship season. The November 19, 1944 edition of the *A-J* reported that Private Ward; his wife, Geraldine; and their eighteen-month-old daughter, Ginger Elaine, visited Lubbock on furlough. Before the war, he worked for the *A-J* for many years as a paperboy, a salesman and in the classified advertising department.

A December 17, 1944 article stated: "Flying with a unit of the Fourth Marine Air Wing, Marine First Lieutenant J.A. Blackwell Jr. recently completed his 25th bombing and strafing combat mission against enemy-held positions in the Marshalls." He was known for his hustle for the LHS team.

The biggest player on the 1939 "Thin Gold and Black" team was 184-pound reserve tackle Carl Sanders. On May 20, 1945, the *A-J* noted he was a sergeant "with a 9th Air Force service command mobile reclamation unit in Belgium and was recently awarded the Meritorious Service Unit Plaque for…superior performance in the repair and maintenance of aircraft" in Europe.

The most improved player on the 1939 Westerners was Frank Redwine, who was assigned to the Sky Lancers, an attack bomber unit of the Fifth Air Force in the Philippines, according to an August 14, 1945 *A-J* article. He was a crew chief "and his knowledge of aircraft maintenance is of great value…in keeping their A-20 Havoc bombers in the air." His wife, Geneva, and eighteen-month-old son, Richard Don, were living in Lubbock with his parents.

A day after the Redwine story ran, the war ended with V-J Day. The Cinderella Kids—except one—returned home. Now scattered from California to New York, the men reunited in Lubbock for decades to relive the unlikely glory of the 1939 championship season.

They hung up their helmets after helping win World War II, and like millions of their compatriots, members of Lubbock High School's 1939 Texas schoolboy football championship team rarely looked back on horrific war experiences. But the Cinderella Kids often reflected on their unlikely football glory in the following decades. Meanwhile, they helped shape the America we know today.

Twenty years after their championship, the players reunited for the first time. In 1959, twenty-four players, managers and coaches came to Lubbock from across the country.

Five team members were gone, joining their beloved coach, Weldon Chapman, who died during that triumphant season. One player could not be located. Six members were unable to attend.

The *Lubbock Avalanche-Journal* reported on the career paths the champions chose. A sampling:

Major Ray McBrayer, USAF, California; Francis Bearden, Rice Institute coach; Dr. L.A. Storrs, Lubbock physician; James Merriman, geologist, Houston; Paul Sparkman, Lubbock sheet-metal business owner; Arlie Chism, brick masonry construction, Lubbock.

Pat Farris, former coach, now salesman for an oil company; Clifton Hill, furniture company, Kansas; Pete Cawthon, Houston banker; Howard Alford,

Lubbock farmer; Leete Jackson, executive vice-president, Red Raider Club; Pritchett Hart, geologist, Houston.

Frank Redwine, Lubbock service station operator; Franklin Butler, art supplies dealer, Lubbock; Jimmy Williamson, automotive parts company employee, Midland; Billy Wright, geologist, Tyler; James Barker, construction, California.

Robert McKinnon, Church of Christ minister, California; Floyd Ward, insurance agent, California; Max Walthall, geologist, Louisiana; J.D. Blackwell, geologist, Louisiana; Dan Gregory, Edmundson farmer; J.D. Milner, editorial staff, *New York Herald Tribune*; Dr. Milner Thorne, Austin physician.

Jack Lovin, who was captured by Germans in 1943, was liberated and became a California physician, but he was unable to attend the '59 reunion.

In 1961, Coach Chap was inducted into the Texas High School Coaches Association Hall of Fame, and his former players attended the ceremonies. The product of a Corsicana orphanage, Chapman graduated from Austin College and coached in Cisco before moving to Lubbock in 1931. His induction announcement said that Chaman brought the double wing formation to Texas schoolboy football and "was a coach's coach, respected by his opponents and loved by his boys."

Meanwhile, "his boys" continued to congregate in Lubbock on a regular basis to celebrate that special 1939 season.

In 1983, team co-captain Leete Jackson reflected on Coach Chap: "When he died, it was like losing part of the family." "We didn't have any stars on the team," Jackson continued. "We just played as a unit. We were just dumb enough to where we didn't think anyone could beat us.

"Everyone's parents tried to make it to the road games," Jackson recalled. "And after we got to winning, you'd notice that the men were wearing the same coats and ties and the women were wearing the same dresses for good luck."

In 1986, back Pete Cawthon remembered, "We won one, tied one and lost three out of the first five non-district games, so it sure looked like we were headed for mediocrity. We weren't cocky; we just knew if we played our game, we could beat anyone."

In 1999, lineman Tom Hart said, "I don't think it's ever happened before or since where a high school team lost its coach like that and went on to win a state championship."

"The thing that was really unusual about our ball club was that we were so close back then and we've hung together all these years," Jackson said.

The 1939 Lubbock High School state champions. *1940 LHS yearbook.*

The last recorded reunion of the Cinderella Kids was on February 24, 2006, when the long-lost 1939 championship trophy resurfaced. Ethyl Storrs, widow of team member Dr. L.A. Storrs, mysteriously came into possession of the prize years earlier. Returning it to its rightful place of honor, she witnessed eight surviving members of the team as they placed the trophy in a case at LHS.

"We're getting so old, we might need to start having (reunions) every six months," quipped eighty-three-year-old Jackson, who was inducted into the Texas High School Football Hall of Fame in 1972.

The history of Lubbock gridiron glory is short. There's a photo in Texas Tech's Southwest Collection labeled "the first Lubbock football team," dated 1910, but that's about all we know of the team. Three years before Texas UIL statewide competition was organized, the 1917 LHS football team went unbeaten and untied, but that's all we know about that team.

Lubbock High School won back-to-back state football championships in 1951 and 1952. In 1963, Lubbock's segregated Dunbar High School won the state football championship in the all-Black Prairie View Interscholastic League. In 1968, Estacado High School won the Division 3 state football championship, the last LISD state championship in football competition.

The Cinderella Kids hung up their cleats and their armor, and their reunions are long over, but the compelling legend of the 1939 Lubbock High School football team will live on in sports history forever.

25

JOE FORTENBERRY

The Forgotten Basketball Hero of Happy

These may be the most obscure of basketball trivia questions: Who inspired the basketball term "dunk"? Who was the captain of the first USA Olympic basketball team? Who prompted the roundball rule against goaltending? Who ended the jump ball rule after each made hoop? What basketball legend has never been inducted into the Basketball Hall of Fame?

The answer to each of these questions is the same: Joe Cephis Fortenberry of Happy, Texas.

Born in 1911, Joe and his family moved from the Denton area to a farm near Happy—population five hundred—when he was fourteen. He spent hours on the family farm, shooting basketballs at a homemade goal. At Happy High School, he excelled in the sport, and by the time he reached West Texas State Teachers College in Canyon, Joe was a dominating, six-foot, seven-inch center, leading the Buffaloes to consecutive twenty-win seasons in 1932 and 1933.

Professional basketball was yet to be invented, but companies under the auspices of the Amateur Athletic Union (AAU) sponsored teams showcasing the best players in the country. Joe went to work for one of those companies, Globe Refinery of Kansas. He led the Refiners to the 1936 AAU national championship, earning an invitation to audition for the first-ever U.S. Olympic basketball team.

Joe's tryout was during the depths of the Great Depression, and the Olympic committee could not pay Joe's way to New York City. Globe refused to finance his trip and threatened that he might not have a job when he got back. Somehow, he managed a ride in a Model A Ford to the Big Apple.

Pulitzer Prize–winning *New York Times* sportswriter Arthur J. Daley witnessed an Olympic workout and chronicled a curious variation of the basic basketball layup by the now six-foot, eight-inch, two-hundred-pound, twenty-five-year-old Texan. "Joe Fortenberry left the floor, reached up and pitched the ball downward into the hoop, much like a cafeteria customer dunking a roll in coffee," wrote Daley, thus coining the basketball term *dunk*, later enhanced as the "slam dunk." The move "left observers simply flabbergasted."

Reflecting on Daley's observation, *Sports Illustrated* writer Michael McKnight wrote in 2015:

Joe Fortenberry. *Public domain.*

> *When Joe Fortenberry, a farm boy from Happy, Texas threw one down at the West Side YMCA in New York City on March 9, 1936, he may not have been the first man to dunk a basketball, but he was the first to do it in an aesthetically stirring way, and in front of the right people.*
>
> *Cameras of that era were too crude to capture the split second when the rules of both Newton and Naismith were bent, so it was fortuitous that the New York Times writer Arthur J. Daley was at the Y that day covering the tournament that would decide which Americans sailed to Berlin for the Olympic debut of the 45-year old sport.*

Joe went on to captain the first USA Olympic basketball team. In Germany, the International Olympic Committee experimented with basketball as an outdoor competition on clay courts. Spain forfeited the first game to the United States, then Joe's team eliminated Estonia, the Philippines and Mexico before facing Canada in the final game. Played in mud during a driving rainstorm, the game was won by the United States, 19–8. Joe was the leading scorer and collected the gold medal.

Following the Olympics, Joe was a four-time AAU All-American, leading his teams to three Missouri Valley AAU titles and the 1940 AAU national championship.

Because of Joe's combination of size, agility and athleticism, AAU basketball rules were altered. Goaltending became illegal because of Joe's talent for swatting away balls just prior to their arrival at the basket. Because Joe seemed to win every tip-off, the rule requiring each possession to begin with a jump ball was abolished.

Joe joined the military at the start of World War II and continued to play basketball on various U.S. Army Air Corps teams. After the war, he went to work as a land man for Phillips Petroleum Company, settling with his wife and three children in Amarillo.

Joe's son Oliver remembered one day he was shooting hoops in the family driveway when his father—about age fifty-five—came home from work. "He had on his overcoat, hat, pipe, slacks and leather shoes," Oliver said. "He took his coat and hat off and said, 'I wonder if I can still do it?' He stood under the goal and dunked it with two hands. His pipe went flying, and he said, 'I don't think I'll do that again.'"

In 1993, Joe Fortenberry died in Amarillo at the age of eighty-two. He had been inducted into the Helms Amateur Basketball Hall of Fame in 1957 and the Texas Panhandle Sports Hall of Fame in 1959. These were worthy honors, but it seems a shame the name of the fellow who invented the dunk is not found in the Basketball Hall of Fame.

26

THE HISTORY OF TENNIS IN LUBBOCK

Doc, dub and Quinn

Football, basketball and other team sports dominate the history of Lubbock athletics. Organized tennis started slow, but tennis has always been an important Hub City pastime.

The earliest tennis court in Lubbock was built at a residence east of town in about 1914. By the 1920s, three public courts were available, one at the Lubbock Inn two blocks west of the post office and two near the First Methodist Church on Broadway.

In March 1922, the *Lubbock Avalanche* reported on improvements to the grounds of the fledgling Lubbock Country Club (LCC). A new clubhouse was planned to include tennis courts and other "plats for athletic amusements for those who wish to go out for a while and do not wish to engage in the national game of golf."

Indeed, LCC's golf, fishing, camping and social activities thrived through the next decade, but the next mention of tennis did not appear until July 8, 1934. A newspaper article announced the "formal opening" of refurbished LCC tennis courts, which had been constructed the summer before. The new courts were "repaired and rolled to almost perfection," indicating the courts were constructed of clay, though grass courts are also rolled.

One of the first local tennis associations was named the Lubbock Lawn Tennis Club in 1924, but there is no evidence a grass tennis court ever existed in the city. Lawn tennis is the proper name for the sport, whether it is played on grass, clay, concrete or synthetic surfaces. By 1938, the LCC courts were constructed of crushed limestone.

Most tournaments in the early 1930s were held at Sunnycourts Tennis Club, 700 Twenty-Eighth Street, or at the Texas Technological College varsity tennis courts southeast of the old Texas Tech gymnasium. Texas Tech first competed in tennis in 1926.

LCC's opening event on July 8, 1934, featured "the best of home talent" exhibition tennis matches under the direction of Lubbock's first tennis professional, Ivan "Doc" Collier. Former city champion W.B. "dub" Rushing, rising local star Henry Roberts and city doubles champions Larry and Renford Taylor were signed for the event. A local newspaper reported the new LCC courts "handled the exhibition play quite well, as a large crowd of spectators witnessed three singles and one doubles match."

Two individuals dominated Lubbock's early tennis history: W.B. "dub" Rushing and Quinn Connelley.

Rushing—who always spelled his nickname in lowercase letters—was a participant in the inaugural LCC tennis exhibition and competed in the first

Quinn Connelley. *Author's collection.*

LCC net tournament later that month. Rushing, Lubbock's ace, lost in the finals of the tournament. But dub, then just age twenty-four, did not allow the bitter defeat to deter his tennis career or his business career. He became perhaps Lubbock's most famous tennis player and promoter of the game and excelled in business.

Rushing played tennis for Texas Tech in the 1930s, opened Varsity Book Store in 1934 and then went on to establish a thriving real estate development business, now known as Lubbock Commercial Buildings Inc. He won countless tennis titles and, at age seventy-three, played a famous Lubbock exhibition match against John ("You cannot be serious!") McEnroe. He played until shortly before his death at age ninety-three in 2007.

Quinn Connelley was a legend in Texas tennis well before he pioneered quality tennis programs in Lubbock in the late 1960s. He was TAAF Men's Singles State Champion in 1932 and coached Rice University tennis for twenty years (1934–54), winning nineteen Southwest Conference titles.

Connelley and his family moved to Lubbock in 1954. He opened a car dealership, Johnson-Connelley Pontiac, at the corner of Main Street and Avenue Q, where he sponsored Elvis Presley's only free Lubbock concert—from a flatbed trailer—attended by future music icons Buddy Holly and Mac Davis.

In 1964, Connelley sold the dealership and became head tennis professional at LCC. His efforts spurred unprecedented interest in the seemingly forgotten sport at both the adult and youth levels. He was recognized as having instigated the youth tennis movement in Lubbock and worked tirelessly to raise funds for new tennis facilities.

Connelley served as LCC tennis pro until his death in 1970 at age sixty-one. Tennis locals credit Connelley with creating the interest in tennis that culminated in the 1972 construction of "The Barn," a state-of-the-art indoor tennis facility, one of the first in Texas.

Challenge cup matches for several years in the 1970s were named in honor of Connelley. In 1995, the first Quinn Connelley Tennis Tournament was held, an open event featuring adult mens' and womens' doubles competitions. Organizer Doug Davis said, "We want to make it in remembrance of Quinn Connelley." The tournament has since been a fixture on the South Plains tennis circuit.

In 1984, Connelley was inducted into the Rice University Athletics Hall of Fame. In 2011, he was inducted into the Texas Tennis Hall of Fame.

27

THE GREATEST BASKETBALL
COACH OF THE TEXAS PLAINS

He is the answer to an obscure pro basketball trivia question and one of the greatest basketball players and coaches in Texas history, but few remember his name: Clifton McNeely.

Born in Greenville, Texas, in 1919, McNeely graduated from Slidell High School in 1937. He was a college basketball star at Decatur Baptist Junior College and Texas Wesleyan University before World War II. Following the Pearl Harbor attack, McNeely joined the U.S. Army Air Corps and played basketball for several military teams.

McNeely returned to Wesleyan after the war to complete his degree in administrative education. During his senior year (1946–47), he became known as "The Man of a Million Shots" and led his team to a school record 30-4 season, a conference championship and All-America honors. The scrappy five-foot, ten-inch McNeely played forward and led the NAIA in scoring with 725 points.

In 1946, the National Basketball Association began as the Basketball Association of America (BAA). The BAA's first player draft was in 1947, and the league's first selection went to the Pittsburgh Ironmen. The franchise chose McNeely, but he had no interest in professional basketball. (Salaries averaged seventy-five dollars a game.) McNeely was one of only two number-one NBA draft picks who never played pro ball.

In 1948, McNeely was hired as head coach of the Pampa High School (PHS) Harvesters. Pampa, a Panhandle town of only fifteen thousand residents, played in Texas basketball's 4A division, which was the league

Coach Clifton McNeely, who led the Pampa Harvesters to four state basketball championships. *Courtesy of the Texas Panhandle Sports Hall of Fame.*

for the state's largest schools. (Pampa still plays 4A, but the largest schools now play 6A.)

McNeely's Harvester teams won state championships four times (1953, 1954, 1958 and 1959). From 1952 to 1955, the Harvesters won 72 straight games. During his PHS coaching career (1948–60), McNeely's record was 320-43, an 88 percent winning rate.

His players loved and respected him. They described him as a legend, a basketball genius, a great teacher of the game, an innovator and a perfectionist. He was a man of faith and a positive role model for his players.

"Coach Mac" was also a disciplinarian. One year, several starters were caught smoking, a violation of team rules. The coach kicked them off the team, and the Harvesters went on to win the state championship.

EJay McIlvain starred on the Harvesters' 1953–54 championship team. "I'll tell you my criteria of a coach," McIlvain said of McNeely. "He's got to relate to the players and be honest with the kids. [McNeely] knew how to deal with each individual player and with the team as a group of people."

McIlvain remembered the coach driving to the rural McIlvain home many times to check on EJay's brother Von, who was dying of cancer. "Coach McNeely…was instrumental in helping me overcome the loss of my brother."

Coach Mac believed playing against better players would make the team better. He arranged practice games against junior college teams. Clarendon Junior College was one team the Harvesters beat in scrimmages.

Bill Neslage remembered his Harvester basketball experience of the late 1950s. The pregame team meals were always light portions of lean beef and vegetables. When a Friday game came along, Coach McNeely noticed Bill was not eating. Bill explained that his Catholic faith did not allow him to eat meat on Fridays. "Coach McNeely ordered a big plate of fried catfish just for me!," Bill said. "Pretty soon, my teammates all claimed to be Catholic," and thereafter, the coach fed the whole team fried fish for Friday games.

Bill's younger brother Bob Neslage remembered his sophomore season under Coach McNeely. "He worked with each sophomore and taught us fundamentals. His goal was to bring out the best in each of us. His demeanor was superb, and if you didn't execute properly you could see the disappointment in his face. Never did I see him criticize a player in a team surrounding. We all sought his approval."

McNeely left Pampa after the 1960 season and never coached again. He became an educator at several Texas high schools before retiring in 1985 as administrator for the Irving Independent School District. His twin sons became basketball coaches. Son Phillip won three 5A state championships as coach of Duncanville High School and was voted into the Texas High School Basketball Hall of Fame.

In 1994, Pampa mayor Bob Neslage, McNeely's former player, presented him with the Outstanding Citizen award as many of the coach's other players watched.

McNeely died in 2003 at age eighty-four. As the coach requested long before his death, former player and Nazarene minister Jim Bond officiated at his funeral.

Former players spearheaded many of Coach Mac's honors, including the naming of Pampa High School's basketball facility the McNeely Fieldhouse and the establishment of the PHS McNeely Endowed Scholarship. McNeely was inducted into the Texas High School Basketball Hall of Fame, the Panhandle Sports Hall of Fame and the Texas Wesleyan University Hall of Fame.

28

RANDY MATSON

Texas' Greatest All-Around Athlete

Under a warm Mexico City sun, a giant of a man stood at the back of a concrete slab, spat at the iron ball in his hand, carefully nestled the sphere beneath his right cheek, assumed his stance and paused a few seconds. Suddenly, with a quick, graceful 180-degree turn and a mighty shove, he released the sixteen-pound shot with a thundering "Aaugghh!"

The throw landed 20.54 meters (67 feet, 4¾ inches) away. It was a pretty good effort, he thought, but 4 feet short of his world record. It was good enough. Minutes later, Randy Matson stood on the winner's stand as the 1968 Olympic gold medal was draped around his neck. He was a long way from home, the small Texas Panhandle town of Pampa.

Born to Charles and Ellen Matson in 1945, Randy's first love was baseball, and he was a Little League All-Star, but poor eyesight hindered his game. Baseball's loss was a win for seemingly every other sport in town.

The youngster was big, tall and powerful from an early age, but he was also quick. He competed in track and bested opponents in the sprints, but he was soon drawn to the field events of shot put and discus. By Randy's junior high years, no one could come close to his throws.

At Pampa High, he participated in football, basketball and track and field. On the gridiron, at fullback, Randy ran fifty yards for a touchdown, helping the Harvesters beat their archrival, Amarillo High, and he made the All-District team. In basketball, the six-foot, five-inch center averaged fifteen points per game, leading the Green-and-Gold deep into the playoffs. He was twice a hoops All-District selection, an All-State selection his senior year.

Randy's high school track career was off the charts. He ran the one-hundred-yard dash in 10.2 seconds and was twice state champion in shot put and discus, earning All-State and All-America honors. In the off-season, Pampa's Kiwanis Club raised money to send him to track meets in far-flung locations as Randy considered higher education choices.

"He was the most modest kid I've ever tried to recruit," remarked one coach. "A really wonderful person." Almost one hundred colleges offered Pampa's gentle giant athletic scholarships. Texas Tech basketball coach Gene Gibson quipped years later, "If I hadn't fed him all those steaks while trying to recruit him, he would never have been big enough to set the records he has."

Texas A&M offered the Pampa boy the opportunity to throw the shot and discus and also play basketball, so Randy became an Aggie. His college career was remarkable. Randy started for basketball coach Shelby Metcalf and dominated almost every shot put and discus competition.

When his nose was not in a textbook, Randy worked on a weight-training program to add bulk and power to his rangy, six-foot, seven-inch frame, growing to 230 pounds.

At an indoor meet at Lubbock's Municipal Coliseum, Randy left fifty-foot throws behind him, launching the shot just over sixty feet, followed by similar efforts elsewhere. It was the beginning of multiple world-shattering records.

Following the end of the semester, the Pampa Health Club became Randy's base of operations. There, he lifted weights in preparation for the 1964 Olympic trials. In the evenings, cars circled the Pampa High practice field where he worked out.

Randy easily made the Olympic team and traveled to Tokyo, where the nineteen-year-old won silver with a sixty-six-foot, three-and-one-quarter-inch heave. Gold medalist Dallas Long said, "Randy has everything—strength, timing, poise, and a great competitive spirit. I'm glad I got my gold medal this time because it's going to be his to win four years from now."

"I hope you're right," Randy said, grinning.

As Randy returned to dominate college competition, a rival coach said, "One of these days, Matson will peel off his warmup and underneath it he'll have on a cape with a big S on his chest. Then he'll fly away and we'll all wonder if we really saw him."

On a spring day in 1965, the now 265-pound superhero heaved the shot at the Southwest Conference Championship. The official measurement was

Randy Matson (*center*), 1968 Olympic gold medal winner. *Public domain.*

a world-record seventy feet, seven and one-quarter inches, three feet better than the old mark, recognized as the top performance in world track history.

After winning gold in the 1968 Mexico City Olympics, Randy was drafted by NFL football and NBA basketball teams, but he declined, briefly flirting with proposed professional track-and-field leagues. He narrowly missed qualifying for the 1972 Olympics.

Returning to A&M, he spent the balance of his career as executive director of the Association of Former Students. Randy retired in 2007. He and high-school sweetheart Margaret Burns live in College Station and have three children and six grandchildren.

Randy was inducted into the Texas Sports Hall of Fame, National Sports Hall of Fame and National Track and Field Hall of Fame, among other honors. Those who claim that Randy Matson of Pampa is not Texas' best all-around athlete are surely wrong.

PART V

A SAMPLING OF TEXAS PLAINS CULTURE

29

A HARD, HISTORICAL LOOK AT LUBBOCK COUNTY COURTHOUSE MONUMENTS

The Lubbock County Courthouse grounds are home to at least five monuments, some more controversial than others. Most folks pass these monuments every working day without paying much attention. Now seems a good time to take a hard, historical look at the monuments, which may give direction to concerned citizens and county fathers in determining whether a monument should stay or go.

THE "CONFEDERACY/T.S. LUBBOCK" MONUMENT

The oldest and most controversial monument, an otherwise unremarkable chunk of pink granite about four feet tall, stands just a few steps beyond the west doors of the Lubbock County Courthouse. The piece is dated 1964, notable because many Confederate monuments were erected across the South during this era. According to the Southern Poverty Law Center, Confederate monuments were placed in public places by local governments to intimidate Blacks and discourage the civil rights movement, which was gaining momentum in the mid-1960s.

The inscriptions are barely legible. The east side of the stone reads:

Texas
In the Civil War 1861–1865
Texas Made an All-Out Effort for the Confederacy after a 3 to 1 Popular Vote for Secession—90,000 Troops, Famed for Mobility and Daring, Fought on Every Battlefront. A 2,000-Mile Frontier and Coast Were Successfully Defended from Union Troop Invasion and Savage Indians. Texas Was the Storehouse of Western Confederacy Wagon Trains Laden with Cotton—Life Blood of the South—Crossed the State to Mexico to Trade for Medical Supplies, Clothing, Military Supplies. State and Private Industry Produced Guns, Ammunition, Wagons, Pots, Kettles, Leather Goods, Salt, Hospital Supplies. Wives, Sons, Daughters, Slaves Provided Corn, Cotton, Cloth, Cattle, Hogs, Cured Meats to the Army, Giving Much, Keeping Little for Themselves.
Erected by the State of Texas 1964

Some information on the monument is historically accurate. It is true that the State of Texas voted overwhelmingly to join the Confederacy and that many Texans joined in the fight, though two-thirds of Texas Confederates remained in the Southwest, away from the larger action east of the Mississippi. There were no major battles fought in Texas. It is true Texas helped supply the war effort.

The final sentence of the inscription, "slaves provided corn, cotton…to the army, giving much, keeping little for themselves," is disingenuous and offensive. Texas slaves never volunteered to serve the Confederacy, and slaves had no legal means to keep anything "for themselves."

It is odd that a Confederate memorial would be erected at our town square, as the Lubbock area had no part in the American Civil War. The South Plains was home only to Comanche people and huge herds of bison in the 1860s.

The west side of the stone reads:

County Named for Texas Confederate
Colonel T.S. Lubbock
1817–1862
South Carolinian. Came to Texas 1835. Indian Fighter, Soldier, Businessman, Member Secession Convention. Went to Virginia Hoping to Fight for South in First Battle of War. Commended for Valuable Volunteer Services as Scout and Reporting Enemy Troop Positions in First Battle of Manassas. Sent to Texas to Raise Regiment for Army of Virginia. Upon

The T.S. Lubbock Monument. *Photo by Chuck Lanehart.*

Organization, the 8th Texas Cavalry—Famed Terry's Rangers—Elected Him Lieutenant Colonel. Went to Kentucky When Terry Was Killed. Rangers Unanimously Elected Him Colonel Till, with Typhoid Fever, He Died Soon after. Buried Glenwood Cemetery Houston.

Indeed, our county (in 1876) and our city (in 1909) were named in honor of Thomas Saltus Lubbock, a Confederate military officer. As a teenager, he fought in the Texas Revolution, and he later joined a Republic of Texas expedition to explore the New Mexico area, claimed by the republic. There is evidence that Lubbock appeared near his future namesake county when his unit encountered hostile Native Americans at Tule Canyon in present-day Briscoe County.

The inscription is accurate regarding his participation in the Civil War and in Terry's Texas Rangers.

Census records show Lubbock owned thirty-one slaves before the Civil War. A dedicated secessionist, Lubbock was a "very strong and zealous" member of the Knights of the Golden Circle, a secret society that promoted an international slave empire. He was, according to one of the men in his regiment, "small and affable, and made a favorable impression on us."

Thomas' brother Francis Lubbock—also a strong secessionist—was governor of Texas during the Civil War (1861–63). Francis supported the largest and most infamous lynching in Texas, the "Great Hanging at Gainesville" in 1862, when forty suspected Unionists were hanged and two others shot. Governor Lubbock publicly applauded the hangings as justice.

The "Lubbock County" Monument

The monument most recently erected—in March 2017—is also the oldest. In 1935, to celebrate the one hundredth anniversary of Texas' independence from Mexico, the Texas legislature appropriated funds to place granite and bronze markers and monuments across Texas to commemorate historic events. In all, 220 markers were devoted to county histories. Each marker—cost not to exceed $150—was constructed of pink granite, approximately forty-six inches in height and topped with a bronze tablet telling the story of the county.

The Lubbock County marker, placed by Division 5 of the Texas Highway Department in 1936, was originally located two miles southeast of Lubbock on Highway 84, although the exact location is unclear. Due to road construction decades ago, the marker was removed to a county storage site. It remained there until 2017, when it was repaired and relocated.

The small monument is a second tribute to the namesake of Lubbock County, Thomas S. Lubbock, discussed above. Located a few feet southwest of the Confederacy/Lubbock monument, the plaque reads as follows:

> *Lubbock County*
> *Formed from Young and Bexar Territories*
> *Created*   *Organized*
> *August 21, 1876*   *March 10, 1891*
> *Named in Honor of Colonel Thomas S. Lubbock 1817–1862*
> *Member of the New Orleans Greys at the Storming of Bexar, Commander of a Company in the Santa Fe Expedition, Member of the Somervell Expedition, Co-Organizer of the Famous Terry's Texas Rangers, 1861.*
> *County Seat, Lubbock*

Notably, the inscription does not mention Lubbock's service to the Confederacy, although Terry's Texas Rangers were a Confederate unit.

The "Gazebo"

Popularly known as the "Gazebo," the most prominent and practical monument on the Lubbock County Courthouse square is made of wood and is used almost daily for weddings, concerts, political gatherings and many other public activities. The small one-foot-square plaque at the western foundation of the Gazebo reads: "This bandstand was built in 1984 in conjunction with the City of Lubbock's seventy-fifth anniversary celebration. It is a replica of a bandstand that stood on the courthouse square in the early days of Lubbock County." The funds to build the gazebo were provided by Lou Dunn Diekemper. The bandstand was built by David E. Hankins, and the plans were drawn by White Associates Architects. The bandstand has become a landmark to the courthouse square and is often used to guide folks to the proper courthouse, as the nearby federal courthouse has no gazebo.

A TRIBUTE TO COTTON

In December 1986, the J.D. Hufstedler family donated *A Tribute to Cotton*, a six-and-a-half-by-five-foot bronze statue depicting a larger-than-life-sized cotton bale, which stands just beyond and to the northwest of the Confederacy/Lubbock monument. The contribution was in recognition of the 1986 Texas sesquicentennial.

> *A Tribute to Cotton*
> *In the Early 1900s, Area Pioneer Farmers Marketed Bales of Cotton on this Site. Today, this Cotton Bale Serves as a Monument to Those Who Made Lubbock County and the Surrounding South Plains the Greatest Producer of Upland Cotton in the World. In 1899, Lubbock County Grew Only 15 Bales; by 1932 It Was One of the State's Leading Producers; by the 1950s Lubbock and Other South Plains Counties Produced Half the State's Production. 1977 Lubbock County Grew a Record 346,000 Bales.*
> *Irrigation Technology, Improved Cotton Breeds, and Area Innovations Made High*
> *Production Possible. Farmers and Scientists Produced Stormproof and Machine-Harvestable Varieties through the Texas A & M Experiment Station in North Lubbock County, Texas. Texas Tech's Textile Research Center Adapted Methods for Textile Mills to Use South Plains Cotton.*
> *Instrument Classing and Electronic Marketing Techniques Also Were Developed in the Region.*
> *The City of Lubbock Became the Center for the South Plains Cotton Industry with Warehouses, a Cotton Exchange, and 3 Cottonseed Oil Mills.*

THE "VICTIM'S MEMORIAL"

Remnants of the "Victim's Memorial" stand on the northwest lawn of the courthouse square. Here, in April 2005, local victims' advocacy groups erected a black granite monument, along with two benches and a sandstone flower garden. The monument carried an inscription: "Justice will not be served until those who are unaffected are as outraged as those who are." The quote was misattributed to Benjamin Franklin and probably originated with Solon the Lawgiver (circa 640–circa 556 BC), statesman of Athens.

Members of the Lubbock Criminal Defense Lawyers Association (LCDLA) were not pleased. LCDLA president Pat Metze, along with members Alton Griffin and Rusty Gunter, led the charge to have the memorial removed. "It encourages people to become enraged," Metze said in a newspaper interview.

Griffin, a former Lubbock County criminal district attorney, told the *Lubbock Avalanche-Journal* he had a great deal of sympathy for victims of crime. "However, our country is based upon the fact that a defendant is entitled to a fair trial. Victims don't have any liberty at all without that."

When the Lubbock County Commissioners Court ignored LCDLA's request to remove the memorial, the organization threatened to file a lawsuit. Within days, the commissioners capitulated, and the monument was demolished. LCDLA members kept chunks of the smashed granite as souvenirs. The benches and flowerbed remain.

Monuments and memorials are curious things. It seems no person or subject deemed worthy of recognition is entirely without warts. We cannot ignore the fact that Texas was a part of the Confederacy, and we cannot ignore the fact our city and county were named for a Confederate colonel. But to publicly memorialize the Confederacy and Thomas Lubbock's participation in the American Civil War is an affront to citizens who rightly condemn the Confederacy as a traitorous regime dedicated to the preservation of slavery. The 1964 Confederacy/T.S. Lubbock monument should be removed from the Lubbock County Courthouse grounds and donated to the Museum of Texas Tech University. The 1936 Lubbock County monument is much less offensive in its description of Thomas Lubbock and does not directly mention the Confederacy or the Civil War. The 1936 monument should remain with the venerable Gazebo, the *Tribute to Cotton* and the remnants of the Victim's Memorial on the courthouse square.

30

HAPPY TO REPORT THE VERIBEST LOCO TOWN NAMES ON EARTH

West Texas is home to great town names, some aptly descriptive, some rooted in history and many just charmingly goofy.

Folks who founded Levelland, the county seat of Hockley County, were obviously very perceptive people, but perhaps not very creative. The place originally called Hockley City was renamed in 1922 to reflect the local topography, which is remarkably, well, level.

The same is true for those who named the county seat of Hale County Plainview, which might have been called Runningwater or Hackberry Grove to reflect the natural beauty of the landscape. Instead, in 1887, town planners chose to emphasize the "plain view" of the countryside.

An Ector County community's single native tree was cut down to make way for a large gas plant. The town had previously been called Caprock or Strawberry, but when locals applied to the authorities for a post office in 1946, they recommended the descriptive name Notrees.

It would seem the founding fathers of Terry County also chose the name of their county seat to describe the drab surroundings, Brownfield. But no! Promoters hoping to enhance the chances of the town becoming the county seat named it after a prominent area ranching family, the Brownfields.

Similarly, Littlefield is named not for its small pastures but for cattleman George W. Littlefield.

Needmore in Bailey County says all one needs to know about the little hamlet. In the 1920s, town promoters simply wanted more settlers. It never happened.

R 2149. Buffalo on Chas. Goodnight Ranch, Goodnight, Texas.

GOODNIGHT
THE HOME OF THE BUFFALO

THE SCHOOL TOWN OF THE PANHANDLE
GOOD BAPTIST COLLEGE AND PUBLIC SCHOOL
GOOD CHURCHES

GOOD LAND, PURE WATER
AN IDEAL PLACE FOR A HOME
LAND IN LARGE AND SMALL TRACTS

CALL ON OR ADDRESS   PRICES REASONABLE
GOODNIGHT REALTY COMPANY, GOODNIGHT, TEXAS

For Cards without advertisement. Address HENRY LAW, Goodnight, Texas

Postcard promoting the Panhandle town of Goodnight. *Courtesy of Cindy Martin.*

Towns reflecting significant history include the tiny village of Goodnight, at the edge of the Llano Estacado in Armstrong County. It was named for iconic cattleman Charles Goodnight, who built a ranch house there in 1887. Goodnight was the dominant resident, establishing a college, church, school and a reserve for American bison.

Goodnight also named the Briscoe County town of Quitaque, which he believed was an Indian word for "end of the trail." According to another legend, the name was derived from two buttes in the area that resembled piles of horse manure, the real meaning of the Indian word. Others say the name was taken from the Quitaca Indians, a name translated by white settlers as "whatever one steals."

The name for the Cochran County town of Whiteface reflects no racial overtones. Whiteface describes the hardy, red-coated, white-faced breed of English dairy cattle that rancher C.C. Slaughter—the "Cattle King of Texas"—brought to the South Plains in the late nineteenth century.

At the turn of the last century, rancher Charles Warren was wandering through his Bailey County property when he stumbled on a rusty old mule shoe. Inspired—the legend goes—Warren named his spread the Muleshoe Ranch. When the railroad came through in 1913, a town sprang up and adopted the name Muleshoe.

Another name inspired by the cattle industry is the Childress County ghost town of Loco, not named for the character of its residents. Locoweed, the Spanish-derived common name for a plant that produces a poison harmful to livestock, was widespread in the area when settlement began in the 1880s.

Happy, in northern Swisher County, derived its name from nearby Happy Draw, so named because cowboys were elated to find water there in the late 1800s. Residents boast of their "Town without a Frown."

In 1926, the town of Mullin in Tom Green County needed a new name because postal authorities said another community shared the name. According to legend, a young lady happened upon the mayor in a grocery store. The mayor asked her opinion of a new name for the town, and she spotted a jar of Veribest Pickles on a shelf. Everyone agreed Veribest would be a fine name for their town.

In 1936, postal authorities rejected Ledwig as the town name for a Lamb County community. It was renamed Pep to reflect the good nature of its residents.

Several legends surround the naming of Earth, in Lamb County, none having to do with extraterrestrials. Some believe the name was submitted to the U.S. Post Office while a sandstorm was blowing. Another story says the locals were proud of their fertile soil and wanted to name the town Good Earth, which was shortened by the postal authority to Earth.

When settlers along Turkey Creek in Hall County applied for a post office in 1893, they named their community Turkey Roost, but postal authorities shortened the name to Turkey.

In 1927, a small community in Martin County needed a post office. Many names were submitted to the postal authorities. But when the name Tarzan came across a bureaucrat's desk, it seems he was a fan of the movie series, which in those days starred Elmo Lincoln as the "King of the Jungle."

Noodle, established in Jones County about 1898, took its name from Noodle Creek. According to folk tradition, the name meant "nothing," signifying a dry creek bed.

31

EARLY DOCTORS AND HOSPITALS OF THE SOUTH PLAINS

D r. William J. Hunt became the South Plains' first physician when he arrived in Estacado in 1881, but when the village of Lubbock was settled a decade later, the town was without a doctor.

In 1892, Cochran County cowboy Henry Jenkins was stricken with pneumonia. He was taken by wagon some fifty miles to Lubbock's Nicolett Hotel. There, he was treated by Dr. James William Carter, who had traveled thirty miles from his base in Crosby County. Dr. Carter could not save the cowboy, and Jenkins became the first Anglo buried in Lubbock.

For a few years, the community of Lubbock depended on the services of Dr. J.H. Wayland, who traveled from Plainview. When Dr. Hunt moved his family to Lubbock from Estacado in 1893, he was probably the first doctor in the tiny village of fewer than three hundred souls. Dr. Hunt died at age seventy-one in 1900.

Meanwhile, advertisements appeared in the weekly newspaper hawking the services of physicians, but none were local, and most were selling quackery and patent medicines. In the September 3, 1898 issue of Lubbock's *Texan Press-Leader*, the following ads appeared:

> *Dr. Purdy of Houston: guaranteed painless home cure for opium addiction.*
> *Dr. H.H. Green's and Sons, Atlanta, new discovery for dropsy.*
> *B.M. Woolley, MD, Atlanta: Opium and whiskey habits cured at home without pain.*

Dr. Williams' Pink Pills for Pale People. A cure for diseases of the blood and nerves, for paralysis, locomotor ataxia, and other diseases long supposed incurable.

An advertisement for Dr. Lee Dye of Plainview did not offer medical services but instead declared he was a "dealer in drugs, books and stationery."

According to newspaper accounts, two Lubbock children died of disease in the fall of 1898. Four-year-old Elsie Acuff "seemed to have a sore throat and suffered considerably. Medical aid was summoned and all possible done to relieve her but to no avail." There was no mention in the news article of the nature of the "medical aid."

Eleven-year-old Lynn Burns suffered "choking fits" and "died…of Putrid sore throat." The newspaper reported, "Drs. Harp Hunt and Wheelock were summoned and all possible was done to relieve the suffering but to no avail."

"Harp" Hunt may refer to Dr. William Hunt. Dr. William Efner Wheelock, father of Frank Wheelock—one of Lubbock's founders—practiced medicine in Lubbock in the 1890s. Dr. Wheelock "suffered serious financial losses in California," according to a newspaper account, and committed suicide in March 1902. He is buried in the City of Lubbock Cemetery.

About the turn of the century, there was improvement in Lubbock's medical care just when it was needed most. Dr. J.A. Pharr, perhaps the only physician in town, served as county health officer. Then, in April 1901, Marvin Cartmell Overton checked in to downtown Lubbock's Nicolett Hotel. Overton, born in 1878 in Kentucky, was an intern at a Louisville hospital who was exploring medical opportunities on the desolate South Plains.

He must have looked quite out of place with his sideburns, moustache, Prince Albert split-tail coat and silk high top hat, which he lost the second day of his visit in a violent sandstorm. Yet Overton decided that on completion of his internship, he would establish his practice in Lubbock.

He received his medical degree from the University of Louisville School of Medicine in March 1902 and returned to Lubbock. He was twenty-three years old.

Dr. Overton arrived at just the right time. Early in the decade, a smallpox scare struck the South Plains. While treating the family of F.A. Anderson, Dr. Pharr contracted the disease. Dr. Overton took Dr. Pharr's place as county health officer. Soon, Dr. Pharr recovered and assisted Dr. Overton and Dr. G.S. Blake in treating an outbreak of smallpox among patrons of the Nicolett Hotel. They quarantined patients at a "smallpox camp" on the outskirts of Lubbock, and the outbreak waned.

Dr. Marvin Cartmell Overton arrived in Lubbock in 1901, just in time to battle an outbreak of smallpox. *Courtesy of the Southwest Collection, Texas Tech University.*

In 1907, a young ranch hand was brought to Lubbock complaining of abdominal pain. Dr. Overton rented a two-room house and performed an appendectomy on a kitchen table. It was Lubbock's first documented invasive medical procedure, and a big crowd gathered for the event.

Early South Plains physicians overcame difficult circumstances to treat patients. Traveling many miles by horse and buggy, doctors carried as many drugs as possible, using a special bag that held forty to fifty bottles and vials. Most doctors carried separate bags designated for surgical instruments and obstetrics.

In the rough-and-tumble farm-and-ranch community, physicians set many broken bones. Treatment of gunshot wounds was common, though most of the incidents seemed accidental, as accounts of South Plains gun battles are rare.

Operations were usually performed in homes, often on kitchen tables, with a member of the patient's family administering the anesthetic chloroform, dripped on a cloth held over the patient's nostrils.

In 1954, Dr. Overton said, "I don't know how I practiced medicine fifty years ago. It's a wonder anybody ever got well." Dr. Overton, educated at the University of Louisville Medical School, began his practice in the back of Lubbock's Star Drug Store in 1902. At age twenty-three, he was perhaps the most qualified of Lubbock's pioneer physicians. More than a century later, Lubbock is known as a dynamic regional medical center, and Dr. Overton's career illustrates how times have changed.

Dr. Overton traveled throughout the sparsely populated twenty-three-county South Plains region by horse and buggy until 1908, when he bought the first privately owned automobile in Lubbock, a white, two-cylinder Buick with no top and no windshield.

After telephone service reached the Plains, Dr. Overton carried a receiver with a long wire attached. He would throw the wire across an overhead phone line so he could contact the operator and check in with his office, saving on the miles traveled between patients.

By 1909 and the arrival of the railroad, Lubbock was becoming a boomtown, attracting a number of physicians. The *Lubbock Avalanche* carried advertising for Drs. R.J. Hall, Robert Jones, W.L. Garland, J.E. Minyard, O.F. Peebler, S.H. Adams, L.G. Oxford and J.A. Craven, among others.

Early South Plains physicians were aware of the need to keep abreast of the latest medical knowledge and technology, as most had been trained at inferior medical schools. Several doctors gathered in 1909 to establish the Lubbock-Crosby County Medical Society, formed primarily for continuing medical education. Several times each year, members met at the home or office of a local doctor. Scholarly papers on medical subjects were presented, which led to spirited discussions. Drs. J.T. Hutchison, W.L. Baugh, O.F. Peebler, M.J. Overton, C.J. Wagner and J.R. Hall were active members of the fledgling organization, filling leadership spots in their effort to improve the practice of medicine on the South Plains.

Meanwhile, the need for more modern medical care was recognized in 1908. Dr. Overton donated two lots at what is now Main Street and Avenue O for the construction of Lubbock's first hospital, established by Drs. J.N. Stoops and G.S. Murphy. The Lubbock Sanitarium and Hospital boasted twenty-two rooms, a library and both electric and gas lights.

The venture failed, so in 1912, Dr. Overton and Dr. Charles F. Clayton opened the similarly named Lubbock Sanitarium in the 1300 block of Broadway. Within a year, Dr. Overton had left the Lubbock Sanitarium and established the Overton Sanitarium in the 1000 block of Texas Avenue.

When the Overton Sanitarium was converted into a hotel, a group of citizens formed the West Texas Hospital Association, which eventually involved 360 investors who raised $125,000 to build a new hospital in downtown Lubbock. The hospital was completed in 1922, and its original staff included Drs. Baugh, Craven, Hall, Stewart, Starnes and Wagner.

As soon as each facility opened, the Lubbock Sanitarium and West Texas Hospital established skilled nurse training, necessary for nurses to be available for Lubbock and other clinics and hospitals as they began to spring up on the South Plains. It was one reason Lubbock became a major medical center.

In 1919, twenty-four-year-old Dr. Julian Thomas Krueger arrived in Lubbock and immediately made an impact. By 1920, he was chief of surgery at the Lubbock Sanitarium. He developed a reputation as an excellent surgeon, performing more successful operations—and in less time—than many surgeons in larger cities. He traveled to the Mayo Clinic for two weeks every year to hone his skills.

What was later to become Methodist Hospital had its beginnings in 1917 when Drs. J.T. Hutchison, O.F. Peebler and A.R. Ponton began construction of a new Lubbock Sanitarium at Broadway and Avenue L. The facility was relocated to Nineteenth Street and was improved and enlarged over the years before being renamed Methodist Hospital in 1954.

Plains Clinic, which opened in 1936, evolved into St. Mary's of the Plains Hospital. Methodist and St. Mary's Hospitals merged in 1998 to become Covenant Health System, the area's largest medical provider.

In 1925, Dr. Overton's love for children took him to New York to study pediatrics. On his return, he announced he would see only patients under the age of twelve. "He went into a sick room one time to see a child and there was a bouquet of carnations there and one of the family offered him one and put it in his lapel," his daughter recalled. From that point on, Dr. Overton wore a pink carnation in his lapel, his trademark. He delivered three thousand babies, mostly in homes without sanitary facilities.

Dr. Overton was the most beloved physician of Lubbock when he retired in 1954. Aside from his celebrated medical practice, he was a civic leader. He served on Lubbock's first city council and the school board and was president of two area banks. The Overton residential neighborhood, Overton Hotel and LISD's Overton Elementary School bear his name. He died at age seventy-seven in 1955.

32

O'DONNELL'S GENTLE GIANT

Dan Blocker

The best fruit is not what falls, but what you have to reach for.
——Hoss Cartwright

Dan Blocker was born elsewhere, graduated from high school elsewhere and was buried elsewhere, but he always called O'Donnell, Texas, his hometown. The windswept cotton community nurtured the talent that rose to fame as Eric "Hoss" Cartwright in *Bonanza*, one of the longest-running and most popular TV series in history.

He was born in 1928 in De Kalb, Texas, to Mary and Ora "Shack" Blocker. The Great Depression struck, the Blockers lost their farm and Dan was age six when the family moved to O'Donnell to open a grocery store. For a time, the Blockers lived in quarters at the back of the store. Young Dan stocked flour and sacked groceries.

Dan was always big—fourteen pounds at birth. He stood six feet tall and weighed two hundred pounds at age twelve. "My daddy used to say that I was too big to ride and too little to hitch to a wagon—no good for a damn thing," Dan joked.

Ironically, the man who rode a horse in the opening credits of *Bonanza* for thirteen years was not interested in riding as a youth. "We got him a horse and saddle one Christmas," his mother said. "And he just wouldn't fool with it at all. His friends were far more interested in the horse than he was." The horse was sold.

Dan is remembered in O'Donnell as a studious youngster. He was active in Boy Scouts, a standout tackle and field-goal kicker on the football field and once single-handedly lifted the rear end of a '47 Plymouth.

He enjoyed boxing and sorely damaged the reputations of many of his elders in amateur boxing matches held in a roped-off area downtown on Saturday nights. "He would take on anyone who came to town," remembered John Saleh, an O'Donnell attorney who handled a good deal of his friend's legal work. "I don't recall him ever losing."

Dan's high school years were spent at Texas Military Institute in San Antonio. In 1947, he arrived on Alpine's Sul Ross college campus as a six-foot, four-inch, 320-pound teenager, holding his mother's hand. She turned him over to the football coach with a typical mother's admonition, "You look after my baby."

He participated in football, track and boxing but was never the great athlete his PR men depicted years later. College friends remembered him as "a jolly giant of a man who was the most amusing buffoon, the cleverest storyteller, the most hilarious and pleasurable person ever to come up the pike."

After earning a degree in speech and drama in 1950, Dan served as an infantry sergeant in the Korean War, where he was awarded a Purple Heart and other military decorations. After the war, he returned to Sul Ross and earned a master's degree in dramatic arts. He taught school in Sonora, Texas, and Carlsbad, New Mexico, before moving to California in 1956 to work on a PhD degree at UCLA. While working as a substitute teacher, Dan began his career as a professional actor in Los Angeles.

The struggling young actor had small parts in numerous TV shows, including *Gunsmoke, The Rifleman, The Rebel* and *Have Gun—Will Travel* before being cast as Hoss in *Bonanza* in 1959.

Described as the "heart and soul" of *Bonanza*, the character of Hoss was a stereotypical gentle giant wearing a ten-gallon hat and a perpetual toothy smile. He brought a warmth and empathy that helped ground the show. Directors described Dan as gregarious and friendly to everyone.

The series ran fourteen seasons, was ranked number one three straight seasons and spent nine seasons in the top five. *Bonanza* is still popular in syndication.

TV star Dan never forgot his hometown. When he returned to big-city Texas for promotional events, he often found time to visit O'Donnell, population 1,200. Once, he rode a horse through town during a parade. His stardom on *Bonanza* made him the darling of his friends and neighbors,

Cast of *Bonanza*, with Dan Blocker as Hoss (*left*). *Courtesy of the O'Donnell History Museum.*

and they had good memories of the studious boy—his nose usually in a book—now on the back of a horse, galloping into their living rooms every Sunday night.

Unfortunately, Dan's local-boy-makes-good story had a tragic ending. On May 13, 1972, he died in Los Angeles of a pulmonary embolism following gallbladder surgery. Dan Blocker was forty-three years old. The writers of *Bonanza* had Hoss killed in an accident in the show's storyline that autumn. *Bonanza* lasted another season without Hoss, and the fourteenth and final season ended on January 16, 1973.

Dan was buried in the family plot in De Kalb beside his father, mother and sister. He was survived by his wife, Dolphia, and four children. His two sons are in show business: Dirk is an actor, and David is a film producer.

33

THE SALVATION
OF THE SETTLES HOTEL

Two things immediately catch the eye when traveling south through the Texas city of Big Spring. The pancake-flat plains suddenly give way to a hilly landscape, and the skyline is dominated by an imposing monolith, a ninety-two-year-old semi-skyscraper in the middle of downtown, the Hotel Settles.

The Settles was once hailed as the tallest building between Fort Worth and El Paso. With fifteen stories, 170 rooms, a restaurant and a pharmacy, it was also considered the most luxurious. A fickle oil industry, declining local economy and neglectful ownership took a heavy toll on the grand structure, but an enigmatic local boy who made good restored the place to spectacular new life in 2012.

Big Spring, on the southern edge of the Llano Estacado, has always been a small but vibrant city. Named after a large spring in the southwestern part of town, the place is officially Big Spring, not Big Springs. When oil was discovered nearby in the 1920s, the town quickly tripled in population. People were living in tents, and proper accommodations were in order.

Howard County ranchers W.R. and Lillian Settles became wealthy through the oil industry and saw the need for a majestic Big Spring hotel. They hired famed Abilene architect David Castle, who designed the concrete art deco edifice, which had a $700,000 price tag ($11.5 million in today's terms).

Hotel Settles opened in 1930, featuring a spectacular marble split-lobby staircase leading to the mezzanine and grand ballroom. Polished marble covered the floors, paneling was mahogany and furnishings were of the finest walnut. Rooms featured "running ice water," and luxury bathrooms were decorated in "Egyptian color schemes of black and white." An eleven-piece orchestra provided opening-night entertainment, with more than three hundred people packed into the ballroom. The hotel manager bragged, "I have no hesitancy of comparing the class, service and beauty of the Settles Hotel with that of the New Yorker in New York City. In fact, I think this hotel is superior in many respects."

Soon, the Great Depression hit West Texas hard, and W.R. and Lillian lost their hotel. A succession of owners followed over the decades, and with a new military base and the oil boom in the 1950s, the hotel flourished as the cornerstone of local activities, wedding receptions, conventions, proms and friends meeting for lunch. The Settles hosted many famous guests: former president Herbert Hoover, Elvis Presley, Lawrence Welk, Gene Autry, Jack Benny and Jerry Allison of Lubbock's Crickets, among others.

Gradually, the hotel began to fall into decline, and by the 1960s, it had been reduced to a flophouse/brothel. In 1980, the Settles closed, and in the ensuing years, it became a decaying eyesore. Locals believed it was beyond repair.

Enter G. Brint Ryan. Born in Big Spring in 1964, he graduated from Big Spring High School and earned accounting degrees from North Texas State University. After a stint with Coopers & Lybrand, he started a tax services firm in Dallas. The company saved billions in taxes for its clients and grew to dozens of locations across North America and the United Kingdom. Ryan became a billionaire, yet almost no one in Big Spring seemed to know much about him. Soon, he would be the talk of the town.

"I just fell in love with the property," Ryan said of the Settles. "It's a phenomenal building, but it was just about as close to total destruction as you can imagine."

In 2006, he bought the Settles for $75,000 and began the renovation process. The roof had caved in and one floor was piled waist-high with dead pigeons. It took a year to remove seven hundred tons of lead paint and asbestos from the structure.

Ryan said he was motivated to undertake the project because of the building's qualities—"an architectural gem"—and the opportunity to participate in an important community project in his hometown. And because everyone said, "Oh no, that can't be done."

Six years and $30 million later, the Hotel Settles reopened in 2012 with sixty-five guest suites, event and meeting spaces, a pool, a fitness studio, the Settles Grill and the Pharmacy Bar & Parlor.

Skyline of Big Spring. *Courtesy of the Hotel Settles.*

Ryan is thrilled with the results. "We restored it as close as possible to the original as you can imagine," he said. "W.R. Settles, if he walked in the lobby today, he'd recognize the place." The renovations took into account the building's original blueprints, and the National Park Service accepted the hotel for its National Register of Historic Places.

Aside from the Settles, Ryan purchased and renovated a number of smaller buildings in downtown Big Spring, including the Reed Hotel and the Petroleum Building.

"The Settles has been a big boom," said Mayor Shannon Thomason in a 2021 interview. "It ignited redevelopment downtown. We will soon have a distillery downtown and a new central plaza with lots of green space. A lot's been done, and there's more coming."

34

THE CONEY ISLAND CAFÉ

Pampa's Iconic Eatery

Woody Guthrie and Bob Wills frequented Pampa's Coney Island Café, and during hard times, both cultural icons washed dishes there. Following a virtuoso piano performance, Van Cliburn dined at Coney Island. Generations of regular Pampa folks have enjoyed the quaint charms of this downtown eatery, the oldest in the Texas Panhandle.

For decades, huge red neon letters flashing "CAFÉ" have invited hungry visitors to a tiny space on West Foster Street lined with colorful counter stools and booths. But the history of Pampa's Coney Island originated much earlier, in the mountains of northern Greece.

The Coney Island hot dog (Coney dog, Coney) is a beef frankfurter in a bun topped with savory meat sauce and sometimes other toppings, often offered as part of a menu of classic American "diner" dishes. The Coney was introduced to the United States in the early twentieth century by Greek immigrants who originally settled in the Brooklyn neighborhood known as Coney Island. (Some claim the Coney originated in Jackson, Michigan, in 1914.)

One Coney pioneer was Greek immigrant Bill Coronis, who stowed away on a steamer, arriving at Ellis Island in the early 1900s. He wandered to New Hampshire and Nebraska and then arrived in the rough-and-tumble Texas town of Borger, where he established his first venture, the Buffalo Café, in 1926. Robbed twice in one week, Bill vamoosed.

He bounced around the Texas hinterlands and soon settled just down the road from Borger in the bustling oil boomtown of Pampa. There, in 1933,

Bill opened a concession in the lobby of the State Theatre on Cuyler Street downtown. Three years later, the concession evolved into a café one block north, at 104 North Cuyler.

As an immigrant, Bill understood poverty and hunger. During Pampa's Dust Bowl / Depression years, he displayed unwavering benevolence toward people beset by tough times. No one hungry was turned away. They were fed, then helped to find jobs to pay their debts.

Folk music icon Woody Guthrie was a patron. He drank many a beer and ate many meals at the Coney during his Pampa years, before his rise to fame. When funds were short, Woody washed dishes and mopped floors there. His Coney experiences inspired a song, "All Alone on Saturday Night."

Bill's nephew John Gikas joined the business in 1946, and in 1951, with Bill's passing, John's brother Ted Gikas became co-owner of the Coney. The café thrived, and they settled into the present downtown location, 114 West Foster, in 1956.

About that time, John got religion and demanded the Coney stop selling beer, sparking a huge argument between the brothers. Ted thought the business would go broke without alcohol sales, but the atmosphere became more family-oriented, and business increased.

Coney Island Café, circa 1940. *Courtesy of Corey Coronis.*

In the following decades, the Coney became a favored gathering spot for camaraderie, jokes and gossip. Movers and shakers of the town—merchants, lawmen, elected officials—hung out at the café even before opening hours to casually chart the future of the community over coffee.

The structure, barely twenty-four feet wide and ninety feet deep, featured booths with rustic wooden seats and bright-yellow table tops on the west wall and a matching counter with twelve red swivel stools on the opposite wall. The red-tiled linoleum floor was accented by an orange ceiling with dark, wood-paneled and beige stucco walls.

Naturally, the simple fare featured Coneys: heated wieners on steamed buns, covered with warmed mustard, piping-hot homemade chili (no beans) dusted with freshly chopped onions, selling for just eighty cents as late as 2000. Other items on the thin menu: chili, hamburgers, stew, soup and a few sandwich selections. The remaining options: twenty varieties of fresh, made-from-scratch daily pies. The popular favorite was Greek-inspired egg custard pie, served warm, which usually sold out before dinner.

The Pampa Fire Station was a couple of blocks from Coney Island. When pies went unsold, the Gikas brothers treated firefighters to the leftovers.

They devised an archaic system of code, barking orders across the room ("One on one! Two on one!"), insisting that servers remember every order and bill without writing anything down, accepting only cash.

The brothers became pillars of the Pampa community. John was deacon of the Baptist church and served as president of the school board. Ted was heavily involved in the arts and nonprofit community projects.

John and Ted ran the Coney Island for more than fifty years, working six days a week from 11:00 a.m. to 7:00 p.m., with a couple of weeks off each spring. When they retired in 2001, the Coronis/Gikas family had operated the eatery for sixty-eight years.

The Donelson family purchased the business, and in 2017, native Pampan Brandon Richards bought the café. Soon, Lupe Martinez joined Brandon in the venture.

"It's been such a big icon of Pampa," Lupe said. "There's so many memories that are made here." Another local said, "It's not Pampa without the Coney Island."

INDEX

D

E

F

M

N

X

Y

ABOUT THE AUTHOR

Chuck Lanehart is a criminal defense lawyer based in Lubbock, Texas. In his forty-five-year career, he has represented citizens accused in almost the entirety of the Texas Plains and beyond. Thirty-plus years ago, he began writing about the rich legal and cultural history of the region. His history essays have been featured in many publications, including legal journals and newspapers. Westerners International honored him with the Coke Wood Award for Best Published Article of 2020. In 2021, The History Press published his first book, *Tragedy and Triumph on the Texas Plains: Curious Historic Chronicles from Murders to Movies*. The *Lubbock Avalanche-Journal* named him among the "200 Most Influential People in the History of Lubbock" in 2008.